D0017782

The Power of Small

THINK SMALL TO LIVE LARGE

Other New Hope books by JENNIFER KENNEDY DEAN

Life Unhindered!: *Five Keys to Walking in Freedom*

Live a Praying Life: *Open Your Life to God's Power and Provision*

Live a Praying Life *Leader Kit*

Live a Praying Life *Journal*

Heart's Cry: *Principles of Prayer (Revised Edition)*

Fueled by Faith: *Living Vibrantly in the Power of Prayer*

Secrets Jesus Shared: *Kingdom Insights Revealed Through the Parables*

Secrets Jesus Shared *Leader Kit*

Legacy of Prayer: *A Spiritual Trust Fund for the Generations*

Riches Stored in Secret Places: *A Devotional Guide for Those Who Hunger After God*

The Life-Changing Power in the Blood of Christ

The Life-Changing Power in the Name of Jesus

The Power of Small

of

THINK SMALL TO LIVE LARGE

JENNIFER KENNEDY DEAN

NEW HOPE
PUBLISHERS

BIRMINGHAM, ALABAMA

New Hope® Publishers
P. O. Box 12065
Birmingham, AL 35202-2065
www.newhopepublishers.com
New Hope Publishers is a division of WMU®.

Library of Congress Cataloging-in-Publication Data

Dean, Jennifer Kennedy.
 The power of small : think small to live large / Jennifer Kennedy Dean.
   p. cm.
 ISBN 978-1-59669-313-5 (sc)
 1. Meditations. I. Title.
 BV4832.3.D43 2011
 242--dc23
                        2011025668

ISBN-10: 1-59669-313-4
ISBN-13: 978-1-59669-313-5

N114147 • 0911 • 4M1

Cover & interior design: Michel Lê
Cover photo: Christine Lê

To my sons- and daughters-in-law:

You give me so many reasons to be proud of you, but let me name a few.

Your compassion and kindness
Your integrity
Your wild and riotous sense of humor

I'll save the rest for another book!

Brantley and Caroline
Kennedy and Sara
Stinson and Stephanie

This is my prayer for you:

"My mouth will speak words of wisdom;
the utterance from my heart will give
understanding" (Psalm 49:3).

Table of Contents

ACKNOWLEDGMENTS

Without the help and encouragement of others, no book could ever come into being and the ministry would be something far less than it is.

New Hope Publishers—the best of the best!

Mark and Regina Beduhn—without whose combined talents and generosity of time I would be overwhelmed and useless.

Terry Trieu—We still benefit from your meticulous work putting structures and systems in place. I know you are always there for the ministry, whenever and wherever.

Priscilla—Sister by birth and friend by choice, always there to step in do some heavy lifting and keep things running smoothly.

INTRODUCTION

Like Alice's adventures in Looking Glass Land (*Through the Looking Glass* by Lewis Carroll), where everything she encounters is mirror-image opposite of what she thought to be true, the kingdom of heaven seems upside down and inside out when we first enter. Learning its biosphere and how to navigate its landscape becomes the adventure that defines our lives.

The way up is down.

The way to life is through death.

The way to greatness is through servanthood.

Kingdom living turns all of the world's platitudes and conventional wisdom on its head. The two are diametrically opposed. The first exposure to kingdom life principles is mind-boggling. It seems that it would require a mind transplant to absorb the absurdity of it.

So, mind transplant it is. When you are born into the kingdom, the kingdom is born into you. Your mind is reformed and regenerated. The old operating system is replaced with a new one. The new operating system runs all the programs differently. Old things have passed away and everything has become new. You have the mind of Christ, and He can make direct deposits from His mind into yours.

He can think His thoughts through your mind. The LORD has taken out your hard-as-rock, stubborn mind and transplanted a mind that is open and living and receptive.

The mind-set of the world tends to value big. The bigger the better. Flashy—sparkly big. So, when you first notice that the kingdom gives small all the value, it takes a while to absorb it. We are so used to being oriented toward big, that the reorientation toward small feels unnatural. But, small is where all the action is in the kingdom.

SMALL IS THE NEW BIG

Think of something big. A mountain? A tree? Get a mental picture of something you call big. Now, consider that it is made up of tiny, tiny atoms. Atoms are made up of even tinier neutrons and protons. Neutrons and protons are made up of elements so small that they can't be seen with the strongest microscope.

No such thing as big. Everything we call "big" is just a whole lot of "small."

Small upon small upon small finally equals big. There is no "big" without lots and lots of small.

Nature, as God created it, is the image of the invisible kingdom of heaven. His creation illustrates the principles of His kingdom. In kingdom living, small matters. Small is the key to big. Choice by choice, act by act, decision by decision, obedience by obedience . . . a large life is made up of a whole lot of small.

Nanotechnology is all the rage. The technology of the future, some say. The possibilities are endless and the power comes from the size of the nanoparticle. It is tiny. The nanoparticle is so small that it can pass through the skin and through the outer layers of organs. Medicine can be delivered by nanoparticle. Skin treatments can be delivered by nanoparticle. Because the delivery system is so small that it can pass through barriers like skin or organs, it can deliver medicines or chemotherapy or vitamins deeper and more efficiently. The power of small in action.

The Word of God, delivered by the Holy Spirit, is—like a nanoparticle—transdermal. It is more than skin deep. The Spirit carries the power of the Living Word deep into the heart and life and transforms from the inside out. Spiritual nanotechnology means that the healing and renewal that might otherwise sit on the surface can be absorbed in the deep and hidden places. It takes the power of small to bring big results.

LIVING LARGE

"I have come that they may have life, and have it to the full," Jesus states in John 10:10. We are created for fullness and abundance. We are designed to bud and flourish. We are constructed so that we crave and pursue big dreams and long to have lasting impact. We want to live large. God wants us to live large. He has designed a huge salvation that we are to live out in our daily lives.

How do we work out the bigness of our salvation? How do we find the full and abundant life we desire? By paying close attention to the small.

It is our common tendency to dismiss the small while we wait for the large. We are likely to look right past the small because we are only interested in the large.

The word translated "to the full" in John 10:10 can mean "excessive." It has the sense of extravagant and overflowing. God has big plans for our lives. He intends for us "exceeding abundantly" more than we intend for ourselves. The big life He has for us is built small by small.

A 28-DAY JOURNEY

I want to invite you to join me for 28 days in an exploration of how the Word of God presents the power of small. You might want to take this journey with some friends, or with a spouse, or a prayer partner. I find that I process things best when I talk them out with someone I trust. I find something about the give-and-take of honest conversation helps me formulate my thoughts more clearly. The feedback and interaction among confidants forces me to clarify ideas I might otherwise leave filmy and vague. The fellowship also gives me accountability. We can hold each other up and cheer each other on. So, I have designed this book so that you can do it alone, but also so that it can easily be used in groups. I want it to fit the rhythms of your life, so I have made every seventh day a reflective day to evaluate, process, and discuss how the 28 days are progressing. Whether you do that alone or with fellow travelers, meeting together weekly, I think you need to stop and steep every now and then. I know I do.

Each day you will find a "small change" suggestion—one thing you can do or incorporate into your life to build a life lived large.

I suggest that you purchase a journal, if you are not already using one. Each day you will find challenges and probing questions to consider. On each seventh day you will have ways to evaluate and record in your journal. Keep a record of your small changes in your journal. You might find the *Live a Praying Life* Journal would fit your needs.

HOW TO USE THIS BOOK

Commit to 28 days. Decide on a time of day and a place where you will meet the Lord and open yourself to His nano-work in your life. Be as faithful to that commitment as possible.

Record thoughts and responses in this book section: Think Small, Live Large on page 169. It will help you nail it down, and will give you a record to look back on.

Consider asking someone or several people to join you on this journey.

Every seventh day, meet with your partner or group to reflect and process. If you are doing the book on your own, take every seventh day to let the Word put down roots as you review and evaluate.

DAY **1**

"The Lord God formed the man
from the dust of the ground and breathed
into his nostrils the breath of life,
and the man became a living being"
(Genesis 2:7).

Let's start at the beginning. When God first created earth and earth's inhabitants, He built intimacy in. Look how the Supreme God, Almighty God, Creator of heaven and earth God took such great care in creating one man. One human being from whom all others—billions and billions and billions of others—would come. Starting small is God's way.

I realized something recently that I had not seen quite so clearly before. It jumped out and surprised me. I was considering that the power of God's Word that created the universe is as powerful now as it was in the beginning. When God says "Let there be," molecules accumulate into matter, atoms bond together into mass, cell fuses to cell and things which were not, now exist. When the breath of His mouth rushes out to vocalize His Word, even the tiniest neutrino is ordered into lockstep with His command.

Then I started thinking about His breath. It takes breath to form a word. Have you ever been with someone whose breathing is compromised? They can't speak easily. Breath is the transporter of words and without breath, words are imprisoned inside the mind and have no outlet. God's breath is the container of His Word.

Then I started thinking about how He breathed the breath of life into the human He created on the sixth day—the pinnacle of His creation. The same breath that carried the word of creation in it. That led me to consider—and here is the picture that took me by surprise—that He created the human differently than the way He created everything else.

Everything else was formed by His Word, but the human was formed by His hands.

As I observed with my imagination how God shaped the human—formed him, molded and sculpted him—I was awed by the intimacy of touch that was being acted out. How God left His fingerprints and His DNA all over the human. How He took the time to tenderly create this Self-expression with His own hands. Down in the dirt, one with the clay from which He sculpted. He made the human from the dust of the earth He had just created. Earthy. He had all the mechanisms necessary for living in earth's atmosphere, but he had no life.

Then—and now the intimacy is stunning—then God breathes.

He leans over this earthy man, covers the human's mouth with His own, and breathes.

The man formed of earth is filled with the life of the heavenlies. Heaven and earth meet, and life as God intended appears. What was not, now had become. When God breathed, He breathed into the human. Not around him, or over him. He breathed the Word into him.

With the Fall, the man who started out earthy—all earth—was once again earthy. When Jesus, the last Adam, appeared in earth's environment, once again heaven and earth met. When the day came for the Word to indwell mankind again, He breathed (John 20:22).

HE STILL BREATHES

All of His careful attention and His laser focus on one person. It is still His way. He breathes into you as He creates and recreates you. Forms you with His own hands. The Potter's hands are shaping you. You are His workmanship—His self-expression. The reason that He gives you such meticulous attention, assembling and arranging the details of your life, is because you are a beginning. From you He will produce fruit that will last, and will produce more fruit, and more fruit until the final day.

Where is He working and shaping your life right now? The little nudges, the longing for something more, the hunger for something deeper. You are clay in His hands. Let Him shape His vessel.

THE SHAPING OF A LIFE

Sandra grew up in an influential family, married a wealthy man, lived in a beautiful home, and had two lovely children. Life was good. She was a strong Christian and loved the Lord with all her heart. She used her material goods in generous ways. Anyone would have thought that Sandra had it all.

Sandra reached a time in her life when she began to feel a little twinge of dissatisfaction, a sense that there was something more satisfying that she had not yet discovered. She tried to determine what it was she was missing. She prayed, she thought, she strained. Finally, Sandra says, "I just leaned into it. I said, 'Lord, I'm here to do whatever you tell me to do.' And I relaxed. I thought, 'God knows how to tell me what He wants me to hear.'"

A big part of Sandra's life was her church. A wonderful, big, affluent, missions-minded church. She never even entertained the thought that God might be calling her from her church family. Over a period of a few years, God gradually worked in Sandra, moving her to a point where the radical call of God became a deep desire in her heart. It began to occur to her that there were many, many churches in areas less affluent than her own that missed out on the kind of opportunities for Bible teaching and discipleship training that she took for granted. There were other churches that had not one single person able to give financially like she could.

Over a decade ago, Sandra and her family left their much-loved church body to join a church where their spiritual gifts and their finances made all the difference. They found quickly that this new body of Christ and these new friends would become as dear and as meaningful in their lives as any church they had ever been part of.

Sandra says that the move introduced them to beautiful believers that life might never have intersected them with otherwise. Many strong believers have thrived and reached amazing goals under their ministry. Young adults who came from generations of despair have blossomed in life through Sandra's caring discipleship.

Sandra allowed herself to be shaped by the hand of the Creator, and let Him breathe His desires and ideas into her heart. One woman. Small change. Big results.

SMALL CHANGE

Be acutely aware and immediately responsive to the smallest inclinations to risk for the kingdom and longings in God's direction. Respond with this prayer: "Breathe!" Let Him breathe into you His desires for you.

DAY **2**

"When I called him he was only one man,
and I blessed him and made him many"
(Isaiah 51:2).

Speaking of Abraham, the prophet Isaiah writes: "Look to the rock from which you were cut and to the quarry from which you were hewn" (Isaiah 51:1). Not only the physical nation of Israel, but also Abraham's descendants by faith, can trace their beginning to one man, Abraham, and one woman, his wife Sarah. God starts small and builds from the ground up.

Isaiah invites those who want to pursue righteousness and want to seek the Lord to watch the process by which one became many. And the irony is not just that Abraham is only one man, but that he is one man who lacks the very thing he needs to father a nation. He lacks a son.

The person who is living a praying life is not circumstance-driven, but Christ-driven; not problem-centered, but Power-centered. Our frame of reference is not what we lack, but what God has. We define our lives within the context of eternity instead of time.

I find it interesting, then, that when Abram, later to be Abraham, is first introduced on the pages of Scripture, he is defined by what he lacked. We first encounter his name in the lengthy lineage recorded in Genesis 11. All the other men were described in terms of whom they begot. Whom they fathered. Abram is described by his failure to father an heir. That's what we learn about him first of all. The narrative tells us that Abram took a wife named Sarai, and that Sarai was barren and had no child (Genesis 11:20). Abram, who was destined to stand front-and-center as the very definition of a living faith, is introduced not as brave Abram, or faithful Abram, or kind Abram . . . just childless Abram. Defined by lack.

Why? I ask. When there were so many other things to say about Abram, why turn the spotlight on the one thing he lacks? I think the reason is that by shining the light on the lack, the Scripture rivets our attention on the cusp of re-creation. We can't look away. How will a God who so directly calls our attention to Abram's greatest sorrow and humiliation, show Himself the life creator? Watch Him work!

Have you noticed this about God? He never avoids the issue. He never spins the facts or brushes reality under the rug. Up Front God. Look how Paul summarizes Abraham's situation: "Against all hope, Abraham in hope believed and so became the father of many nations, just as it had been said to him, 'So shall your offspring be.' Without weakening in his faith, he faced the fact that his body was as good as dead—since he was about a hundred years old—and that Sarah's womb was also dead. Yet he did not waver through unbelief regarding the promise of God, but was strengthened in his faith and gave glory to God, being fully persuaded that God had power to do what he had promised" (Romans 4:18–21). God just puts it out there. The bad news is setting the stage for the good that is about to come.

It's like He's calling our attention to the need so that when the supply is revealed, we won't be focused elsewhere and miss the power display. Abram's lack has a starring role in the eternal drama. Playing opposite the power and provision of God, Abram's need offsets the wonder of God's plan so that we are nearly blinded by its luster.

As if in Abram's lack, God is saying, "Right here! This is exactly where I am about to apply My power. Take a good look. See the barren, sterile, dried up dream? See the death of hope? Right here is where I'm working!"

Resurrection God. From Abraham—as good as dead—and Sarah—whose womb was also dead—came Isaac. Laughter. Joy. Merriment. Celebration. Life that came from death—resurrection.

Paul calls Him "the God who gives life to the dead and calls things that are not as though they were" (Romans 4:17). Are these two descriptive phrases two ways of stating the same thing? I think so. These words are presented to us within Paul's description of the miraculous birth of Isaac.

Life that came out of death. Paul says the He "calls" those things which are not as though they were. Call can mean to call aloud, utter in a loud voice, invite; to call by name. When did Jesus "cry out in a loud voice" and bring life out of death? John 11:43, as He stood at the grave of Lazarus. "Lazarus, come out!" Called out loud.

I think the Scripture is saying that God steps right into the middle of mucky, messy death—all-hope-lost death; no-way-out death; not-gonna-happen death—and He calls, "Life, come out!" And the voice of the in-the-beginning God reproduces the earth's opening act. He calls order out of chaos. He calls something out of nothing. He calls life out of death.

The lack sets the stage for the provision. Death lays the groundwork for resurrection.

In your praying life, is there a big, hot light on your need? Does it seem to define you right now? You don't have to pretend it's not there. In fact, show it off. That's where God is about to apply His power.

HIGHLIGHTING **RESURRECTION**

Jim grew up in foster homes. He has no memories of his own parents. Through his life as a foster child, he had both good and bad experiences, but always he remembers knowing he was an outsider. He longed for his very own family and to be loved completely. He grew up to marry June, a woman who loved him like he had always longed to be loved. They have a son, the light of their lives. They had hoped to have more children, but after years of trying, concluded that it was not to be.

Jim loved his family and took extraordinary delight in the life he had built. But, every time he remembered his years in foster care, he thought about other children experiencing the transitory life of a minor caught up in the foster system. Together, he and June decided to become foster parents. Ten years later, 15 children have spent some years of their lives in Jim and June's loving home. They have loved and nurtured and disciplined and guided 15 lives. They take great joy in knowing that these lives have likely taken new directions due to the call God had on their lives. Jim knows that his own lack of committed love and family during his youth has made him a better foster father. "I try to give the kids just what I wished someone would give me when I was their age. I learned how to love by not being loved."

SMALL CHANGE

When you think about what you lack, instead of resenting it, let it be a platform for God's power and provision in your life. When the anxiety or the longing sweeps you into its orbit, pray this: "Yours."

DAY 3

*"I will make you into a great nation and I will
bless you; I will make your name great,
and you will be a blessing"
(Genesis 12:2).*

Before God's call to Abraham, several people had been sent from their land. People before Abraham had been called from a land. But Abraham's call was a call toward a land.

It's true, that Abraham must come away and leave behind the land of his birth so he can grasp the land of his promise. That surely required wrestling at the deepest places. The tendency of our human nature to hold onto what is familiar is well documented. But, the clarion call innate in the command was a call to a new place, a call to a promise. The command to leave behind was tangential to the promise of a land to possess. It always requires a crucifixion to experience a resurrection.

Abraham was one man. He lived in a bustling, populous region teeming with men. Why doesn't God reveal Himself to the city? Or, at least the whole clan? But He doesn't. He chooses Abraham, and pursues Abraham. As Abraham's life was being transformed by this call, no one else knew anything was happening. It wasn't front page news. To all appearances, life was just moving on as it always did. All the while, inside one man, unnoticed by the world at large, the ground was shaking and everything was being thrown off balance. Inside one man, a monumental change was taking place—a change that would reroute the course of history and set redemption's plan in motion. A small, invisible beginning.

Notice the construct of the call. "Go to a place I'll show you." It is vague and lacks any definition. "Head out that way and I'll let you know when you're there." He left Abraham in the kind of uncertainty that we resist with all our might. Abraham is sent out to wander (Genesis 20:13). Called to a journey that is unmapped, undefined, marked by its very indeterminacy.

Intentionally so, I think. Designed to feel like wandering. Why didn't God map it out? Why didn't He say to Abraham, "Here is where you start and here is where you end"? The way God planned it, if Abraham had any hope of landing on the promise, the journey would require a desperate dependence on the present voice of God. Every step matters because every step is carrying Abraham to the promise and the provision of God. At every little step, Abraham has to be listening because who knows when the next step is the one where God says,

"You're there!" Step by step, little by little, obedience by obedience. A whole lot of small.

What did Abraham's obedience look like? Put one foot in front of the other. Take the next step. Don't try to project several steps down the road. Slow, steady, small.

Look what happens to small when the Holy Spirit is involved. One small step becomes a stride. Your best effort, under His power, becomes His best effort. I think of it like this: Have you ever walked on a moving sidewalk? You take a step and you wind up several steps further because the moving sidewalk carried your small, ordinary step with its forward-moving power. Take that same step without the moving sidewalk and you have progressed one step. Take it on the moving sidewalk and that step has been carried in the power of the sidewalk.

An obedience that might look small and insignificant in the moment will reveal itself later to have been pivotal. Lack of obedience at that moment would have changed everything. Obedience by obedience. A whole lot of small adds up to large.

AN **OVERNIGHT** SUCCESS

Steven Furtick, pastor of Elevation Church near Charlotte, North Carolina, tells the story of his church in the book *Sun Stand Still*. As a 24-year-old married father, Furtick sensed God's call to go to Charlotte, North Carolina and start the church he had been envisioning since his teen years. Why Charlotte? Why Steven? Why now? Furtick didn't attempt an answer to those questions. In obedience to the Lord's call, he and eight other families sold homes, quit jobs, and moved across country. Elevation Church opened its doors with 121 people in attendance, and shortly were breaking records for both attendance and baptisms, currently averaging 8,000 plus in attendance.

The church seems like an overnight success, but it really began years earlier in the small obediences that Furtick learned to live out. The vision grew obedience by obedience, Furtick listening along the way, until the call came for which he had been groomed since his youth. "Leave everything you know and head out this direction." Something like that, I think.

http://www.elevationchurch.org/pastor

OBEDIENCE BY OBEDIENCE

Abraham's journey was begun in obedience and it was carried out daily in one obedience after another. Each time that Abraham came to a moment of risky obedience, the vague vision God has entrusted to him took on more substance. Abraham is to go to a land that God will show him. God will bless him and make him into a great nation. Abraham knows no more than that. He has no clear picture of the mature plan, just an embryonic vision. But he left, as the Lord had told him.

When Abraham reaches a certain place in Canaan, the Lord appears to him. This time He was a little more specific. "To your offspring I will give this land," He said in Genesis 12:7. The vision was taking clearer shape. It had moved from "a land I'll show you" to "this land." In chapter 13, verses 14–17, Abraham has given the vision time and nourishment, and God fleshes it out further.

> "Lift up your eyes from where you are and look north and south, east and west. All the land that you see I will give to you and your offspring forever. I will make your offspring like the dust of the earth, so that if anyone could count the dust, then your offspring could be counted. Go, walk through the length and breadth of the land, for I am giving it to you."

God lays out the boundaries of the land. Furthermore, He expands on His promise to make of Abraham a great nation. He clarifies that the vision is not only qualitative greatness, but numerical greatness.

Abraham has a problem—at least he thinks he does. God has given him the vision of fathering a great nation, but Abraham doesn't even have one son. Abraham expresses his concern.

> "O Sovereign LORD, what can you give me since I remain childless and the one who will inherit my estate is Eliezer of Damascus? . . . You have given me no children; so a servant in my household will be my heir" (Genesis 15:2–3).

Notice how Abraham states his analysis. He says, "You *have given* me no children . . . a servant *will be* my heir." Abraham thinks it's too late. He sees only one way for God to bring the vision about: He'll have to use Abraham's servant, Eliezer of Damascus. In response, God gives Abraham more detail of the vision, a detail He had not yet stated. "'This man will not be your heir, but a son coming from your own body will be your heir.'" The vision continues to take on clearer form.

In Genesis 15:13–16, God fills in more details. For the first time He tells Abraham that his descendants will be strangers in a country that will enslave them for 400 years, but afterward they will come out with great possessions. In the fourth generation, God says, Abraham's descendants will return to the Promised Land. Then, in verses 18–21, God adds more specifics. He gives clearer boundaries of the land of the vision.

> "To your descendants I give this land, from the river of Egypt to the great river, the Euphrates—the land of the Kenites, Kenizzites, Kadmonites, Hittites, Perizzites, Rephaites, Amorites, Canaanites, Girgashites and Jebusites."

The vision has progressed from "the land I'll show you," to "this land" to the detailed description above. Progressive vision. Each step of obedience opening up new dimensions, new understandings. One step makes the next step clear. Step by step, following the Voice that grows the vision.

Finally, God appears to Abraham when he is 99 years old. In the physical realm, Abraham still has no heir. Yet God says, "'No longer will you be called Abram; your name will be Abraham, for I have made you a father of many nations'" (Genesis 17:5). Do you see what God said? "I *have made you* a father of many nations." Before that, God had said "I *will make you* a father of many nations." In the spiritual realm, the work is done. The only thing left is for spiritual truth to be manifested in the material realm. In verses 6–14, God sets forth the terms of the covenant. He gives Abraham a sign of the covenant in the flesh—circumcision. He tells Abraham clearly that not only will the heir come from his own body, but from the body of his wife Sarah. He says, "'My covenant I will establish with Isaac, whom Sarah will bear to you this time next year'" (Genesis 17:21). Now the vision is full-term. It is ready to be born on the earth.

The birth of Isaac was the key to everything God had promised. The birth of Isaac was huge. But it was the result of a whole lot of small.

SMALL CHANGE

Today, celebrate every moment of small obedience. Note it. Value it. Embrace it. In those moments when you choose His way and obey in the smallest detail, let this be your prayer: "At Your service, Lord."

DAY **4**

"But God chose the foolish things of the world to shame the wise; God chose the weak things of the world to shame the strong"
(1 Corinthians 1:27).

Sometimes small isn't about size, but instead has to do with esteem. Things and people held in low esteem are small in our eyes. Unimportant. Valueless. Scorned.

One of the defining characteristics of God's work in the world is the preposterous way He insists on using those we think of as foolish and weak. It seems to be one of His eccentricities—this determination to show the worth of things thought small.

Take Hagar. The narrative of Scripture usually attaches to her name an identifier. Something like "Hagar, the Egyptian slave." She was Sarah's servant and, at her mistress's command, bore Abraham a son name Ishmael. Fourteen years passed during which Sarah remained childless and Ishmael lived as the favored and adored son.

Let's fast-forward to the incident recorded in Genesis 21. Isaac is being weaned. This would likely put Isaac at the age of 5 and Ishmael about 17 years old. Notice this about the telling. Two events play out at the same time. A big boisterous joyful party is being held to celebrate Isaac. Concurrently, Hagar and her son Ishmael are being thrown out into the wilderness. And which scene does the Scripture highlight? The grand celebration? Or the Egyptian slave woman and her son, sent away into the raw wilderness, alone, rejected and weak?

Who would have guessed? The celebration of Isaac gets a scarce mention before our attention is brought to bear on the lowly, rejected, and despised. While we celebrate the winners, God is calling the losers. My son Brantley writes about the dichotomy of this scene:

> *I remember the thrill of October baseball as a young child growing up in Atlanta. So many angst-filled nights were spent alongside my dad and my brothers rooting for the underdog Braves. Any team that faced the Braves back then were to us a hated Goliath, against whom our heroic Davids must battle (this is before Braves solidified their role as the Goliaths of the NL East—often with equally disappointing results!) I remember that GLORIOUS night when the Braves were down in the ninth with two outs and announcer Skip Caray told us that some unknown, untested pinch hitter named "Francisco Cabrera" would be our last hope for*

victory against the Pirates. In the next few moments, as the aged
and hobbled player Sid Bream rounded third for the winning slide
into home, and my brothers, my dad, and I whooped and hollered
like madmen, were pure ecstasy.

My mom happened to be sharing the moment with us and,
noting the devastation on the Pirates' faces—some of them not
leaving the field for many minutes—she dared bring empathy
for the enemy into the midst of our wild celebration of victory!
"Oh . . . I just feel so bad for those other players." HOW DARE
SHE! Clearly, Mom does not understand baseball. This is what
happens: winners and losers. You can't feel for the losers! There
is no time, no place for something so wishy-washy! We must only
rejoice with the winners!

And, so, perhaps others of us would respond to Hagar as my
brothers, dad, and I responded to the Pittsburgh Pirates: the
victory of faith can only be black and white, glorious winners and
deserved losers. To stand UP for faith, even if done by standing
ON another, is the nature of the beast; in this world, this is the
game we play, Hagar!

However, the nature of this story is not the celebration of
Sarah's faith; rather this text, like my mother, enters into our
righteous exultation of the divine promise and calls our attention
to the losers! For us, this story reads as though the camera,
rather than training its eye on the home-plate celebration of the
Braves, zooms in on the faces of each Pirates player as he walks,
defeated, through the clubhouse. Here we are met by the text's
vivid recounting of Hagar and Ishmael's wandering. This story
does not let us go so easily. This text is demanding that we leave
the celebration of home and sit down alongside those left defeated
in the wilderness.

Years earlier, during Hagar's pregnancy, she had found herself cast out
into the desert, driven there by Sarah's harshness and jealousy. As He
would do again later, God seeks her out when she is alone and loathed.
God chooses the wilderness and the slave woman and the outcast son as
the setting in which He reveals a previously unnamed and astonishing
aspect of His character. Here among the small and despised the One
who revealed His name in the past to Abraham—father of a nation—

now reveals His name to little, lowly Hagar. The honor is bestowed on the least likely. Hagar calls Him *El Roi*, the God Who Sees. She doesn't mean a god who glances, or notices in passing. She means the God who sees when she thought no one knew she existed. The God who sees when everyone else has turned their backs. The God who sees when everyone else has averted their eyes. The God Who Sees. When Hagar finds herself again cast out, *El Roi* finds her again. The God Who Sees opens her eyes to reveal His provision. "Then God opened her eyes and she saw a well of water" (Genesis 21:19). He has provision and promise for the discarded and forsaken. "God was with the boy as he grew up" (Genesis 21:20). He not only sees, He seeks out, pursues, and protects.

And the God Who Sees calls us to see. See Him work among the outcasts and the alienated. See Him love the downtrodden and the despairing. See the small because that is where God is doing a big work. See those who are invisible in our world.

SEE THE DUMPING GROUNDS

Author Mary Hollingsworth tells me this story about her friend Beverly, whose idea bloomed from a garbage dump.

> Beverly had worked for Child Protective Services (CPS) in Texas for many years and truly had a heart for hurting children. On many occasions, she had rescued abused children from their abusive parents and placed them in safe homes with foster parents.
>
> In the summer of 2010, Beverly was asked to participate in a missions outreach trip to the famous "dump" in Central America where starving children and their parents literally live in a huge garbage dump, fending for meager food and their very survival.
>
> Beverly felt called by God to make the trip, but she

didn't have the kind of funds necessary to pay for such a costly journey. After praying earnestly about the opportunity, she confided in some of her close Christian friends about the trip, and soon the money for the trip and more came in.

During her days in the dump, Beverly's heart was broken by the barefooted children in threadbare clothes she saw roaming around in the fly-covered garbage, looking for small morsels of food, desperately in need of clean water to drink, with no shelter, fighting off huge vultures vying for the same food they were, and with little prospects of long-term survival.

Each day she watched mothers bring one egg from their small flocks of chickens to exchange for a portion of flour, rice, and water. The egg was used to feed starving orphans. But the women only had flimsy plastic bags, or no bags at all, in which to carry the precious food back to their hovels. The plastic bags often tore or broke, spilling the life-saving food onto the ground. And that gave Beverly an idea!

When she returned home, Beverly told her friends about her trip and about the flimsy bags. Then she asked her friends to purchase a few sturdy, cloth recycling bags and give them to her. She soon collected enough bags to send to the permanent missionary at the dump to hand out to the regular dump dwellers. That allowed the people to safely carry their food allotments home to share with their families. It didn't seem like much of a sacrifice to Beverly and her friends, but it was a great help to the women who had little. The effort was so successful that Beverly continues her "bag mission" today, regularly sending bags to the dump to help the hurting.

Beverly began with very little except a willing heart and a tear in her eye, but she gave God what she had, and He multiplied it to His own glory and to benefit the poor people He loves so much.

SMALL CHANGE

Watch for those in your world who have been invisible to you, whose needs you have not considered. Ask the Lord to cause you to see what He sees. Pray this: "Open my eyes."

DAY 5

*"At that time the Canaanites were in the land.
The LORD appeared to Abram and said,
'To your offspring I will give this land'"
(Genesis 12:6b-7).*

Imagine with me. Abraham and Sarah and the small band of servants began a trip from Haran toward the land God would show them. A land they were to possess. They had livestock and possessions to corral along the way. The journey was long, though there is no clear indication how long. There was the uncertainty of their destination, surely a stress from time to time. In any group of human beings thrown together for a prolonged time, I have to imagine there were arguments and personality conflicts. There were hurt feelings and disagreements. But they were headed toward a promise, so faith and hope fueled their journey and propelled them forward.

Along the way, they found rest in villages and cities, but much of their travel was through unoccupied land. Long stretches of unpopulated land, there for the taking. On they journeyed, Abraham listening for that voice to say, "Here!" On the way to the promise, I imagine that Abraham had times when he said, "Lord! How much longer could it be? Wouldn't this work?" But he kept moving.

When Abraham reached the land that was to be his, do you think it might have been a surprise that it was already occupied? It was the home to many tribes and people. We meet them in the pages of the Scripture. Hittites and "Hizzites" and all kinds of other "ites." There were cities with walls, and commerce, and civilizations, and agriculture. There were armies and governments and places of worship. When Abraham reached his land, it was already taken.

You can see how crucial it was for Abraham to be listening to God because otherwise he would have walked right on past the promise. It didn't look like he expected it to look. He would not have recognized it on his own.

> Abram traveled through the land as far as the site of the great tree of Moreh at Shechem. At that time the Canaanites were in the land. The LORD appeared to Abram and said, "To your offspring I will give this land." So he built an altar there to the Lord, who had appeared to him (Genesis 12:6–7).

Abraham never owned any plot of land in Canaan until he bought land in which to bury Sarah. He lived as a stranger and alien in the land that the Lord said was his. This remained the case for three generations. Abraham fathered Isaac, who fathered Jacob and Esau. Jacob fathered 12 sons, one of whom was Joseph. At this point in the history of the lineage of Abraham, the precursor of a great nation, here is how the Scripture describes them as they lived in the land promised to them:

> "To you I will give the land of Canaan as the portion you will inherit." When they were but few in number, few indeed, and strangers in it, they wandered from nation to nation, from one kingdom to another (Psalm 105:11–13).

> By faith Abraham, when called to go to a place he would later receive as his inheritance, obeyed and went, even though he did not know where he was going.
>
> By faith he made his home in the promised land like a stranger in a foreign country; he lived in tents, as did Isaac and Jacob, who were heirs with him of the same promise (Hebrews 11:8–9).

Abraham left his home and his family, wandered in uncertainty until he reached the borders of Canaan, only to find himself in a situation filled with more uncertainty, more ambiguity. He had left behind stability and certainty and a life with clear outlines. He arrived at the promise, thinking he would be the owner and the ruler and the master, to discover that he would be a stranger and a wanderer.

What did Israel—the promised great nation who would someday be many millions strong—look like at its inception? Small.

When in Jacob's lifetime a famine forced the nation of Israel into exile in Egypt, the nation of Israel had about 75 people in it. When they left Egypt 430 years later, some estimates are as high as between 2 and 3 million, but certainly an astonishingly greater number than entered Egypt, left Egypt.

After their 40-year experience in the Sinai Desert, they took possession of the land in which their forefathers had wandered as strangers. One city at a time. Battle by battle, obedience by obedience, they conquered the occupiers and laid claim to the promise.

Where was God in the interim? What was He doing to get all the details in place for the promise to be revealed in their lives? He was working on both sides of the situation. He was building a strong nation, numerous and skilled. Their skills at building and carving and weaving and everything else they would need to know, as well as their physical strength and stamina, all developed in their experience as slaves.

At the same time, He was working in Canaan, preparing the ground so that when He brought them back, everything would be ready.

> When the LORD your God brings you into the land he swore to your fathers, to Abraham, Isaac and Jacob, to give you—a land with large, flourishing cities you did not build, houses filled with all kinds of good things you did not provide, wells you did not dig, and vineyards and olive groves you did not plant—then when you eat and are satisfied, be careful that you do not forget the Lord, who brought you out of Egypt, out of the land of slavery (Deuteronomy 6:10–12).

> "So I gave you a land on which you did not toil and cities you did not build; and you live in them and eat from vineyards and olive groves that you did not plants" (Joshua 24:13).

He was putting provision in place. All the time the Israelites were slaves in Egypt, and wandering in the desert, God was preparing a land of rest. All kinds of activity was happening on their behalf. Cities being built, vineyards being planted, wells being dug. The promise was in progress even when it looked to them like God had forgotten them. When they were small and helpless, He was moving them step by step toward the large life He had for them.

He was preparing in yet another way. Remember the giants who lived in the land? Remember how Moses' spies described the situation after their reconnaissance mission?

> But the men who had gone up with him said, "We can't attack those people; they are stronger than we are." And they spread among the Israelites a bad report about the land they had

explored. They said, "The land we explored devours those living in it. All the people we saw there are of great size. We saw the Nephilim there (the descendants of Anak come from the Nephilim). We seemed like grasshoppers in our own eyes, and we looked the same to them" (Numbers 13:31–33).

They still viewed themselves a small. They compared themselves to the obstacle in their way and pronounced themselves "grasshoppers." They felt like grasshoppers and assumed that everyone saw them the same way.

If only they had instead compared the size of the obstacle to the power of God. How different everything would have looked then. They didn't know that God had already defeated their gigantic enemy and that they were ready to fold at the first sign of Israel's approach. Here is how Rahab explained it 40 years later when Joshua sent in two spies in preparation for taking the land.

[Rahab] said to them, "I know that the LORD has given this land to you and that a great fear of you has fallen on us, so that all who live in this country are melting in fear because of you. We have heard how the LORD dried up the water of the Red Sea for you when you came out of Egypt, and what you did to Sihon and Og, the two kings of the Amorites east of the Jordan, whom you completely destroyed.

"When we heard of it, our hearts melted and everyone's courage failed because of you, for the LORD your God is God in heaven above and on the earth below" (Joshua 2:9–11).

God's call is always to live large. When the journey has us small, God is still huge. Every step we take in response to God is a building block. Never wasted effort. Never lost time. Every small obedience is the key to living large. While we keep our eyes on the next step, God is working beyond our sight doing things we can't imagine, preparing the promise for the taking.

SMALL CHANGE

Keep obeying even when it looks to you like God is absent. When your thoughts turn toward those places where you can't see God moving, pray this: "Thank You for what You're doing."

DAY **6**

*"He gave you manna to eat in the desert,
something your fathers had never known,
to humble and to test you so that in the end
it might go well with you"
(Deuteronomy 8:16).*

Moses is reviewing with the people how God's care has been evident as they wandered through the desert toward the promise. Read it for yourself.

Remember how the LORD your God led you all the way in the desert these forty years, to humble you and to test you in order to know what was in your heart, whether or not you would keep his commands.

He humbled you, causing you to hunger and then feeding you with manna, which neither you nor your fathers had known, to teach you that man does not live on bread alone but on every word that comes from the mouth of the LORD.

Your clothes did not wear out and your feet did not swell during these forty years.

Know then in your heart that as a man disciplines his son, so the LORD your God disciplines you.

Observe the commands of the LORD your God, walking in his ways and revering him.

For the LORD your God is bringing you into a good land—a land with streams and pools of water, with springs flowing in the valleys and hills;

a land with wheat and barley, vines and fig trees, pomegranates, olive oil and honey;

a land where bread will not be scarce and you will lack nothing; a land where the rocks are iron and you can dig copper out of the hills.

When you have eaten and are satisfied, praise the LORD your God for the good land he has given you.

Be careful that you do not forget the LORD your God, failing to observe his commands, his laws and his decrees that I am giving you this day.

Otherwise, when you eat and are satisfied, when you build fine houses and settle down, and when your herds and flocks grow large and your silver and gold increase and all you have is multiplied, then your heart will become proud and you will forget the LORD your God, who brought you out of Egypt, out of the land of slavery.

He led you through the vast and dreadful desert, that thirsty and waterless land, with its venomous snakes and scorpions. He brought you water out of hard rock.

He gave you manna to eat in the desert, something your fathers had never known, to humble and to test you so that in the end it might go well with you. You may say to yourself, "My power and the strength of my hands have produced this wealth for me." But remember the LORD your God, for it is he who gives you the ability to produce wealth, and so confirms his covenant, which he swore to your forefathers, as it is today (Deuteronomy 8:2–18).

The people had some trying times. Desert years are no picnic. In those years, though big in population, they were small in power. No land. No home. No houses. No fields of their own. Like the patriarchs before them, they were living in tents and wandering. They wandered in circles with the Promised Land just out of reach.

Yet, when they looked back, they could see the hand of God ever-present. In the moment, they found plenty to grumble about as they journeyed. They did not always feel the presence and power of God as they wandered. But in hindsight His provision was clear.

Did they think they were wandering? Hindsight revealed that God was leading them. Did they think they were deprived because they lived with a day's provision at a time? Hindsight revealed that daily provision meant they were rich and well supplied. Did they feel that they had to wear the same old clothes for years and years? Hindsight revealed that their clothes stayed new, so really they had new clothes every day. Did they resent the long, arduous walk through "that vast and dreadful desert, that thirsty and waterless land"? Yet, hindsight reveals that with all that walking, their feet never swelled. They might have been carried, as far as the condition of their feet goes.

In those years, for the most part, they repeated the same obedience day after day with no hint that it really mattered. Manna, quail, cloud, fire. Worship, offer sacrifices, pack, unpack. Set up camp, take down camp. Over and over. No change on the horizon. No evidence of the Promised Land anywhere in sight. Obedience by obedience, they followed the Lord. Small acts of faithfulness every day for 40 years.

As Moses recounts it and refreshes their memories, he doesn't soft-soap the hard edges. It was tough. It was vast and terrible. He reminds them how it felt because they are about to enter the Promised Land and leave the thirsty and waterless land behind. The abundant living in the Promised Land has been prefaced by the long walk in the dry desert. Why?

During their extended training in the desert, they learned by experience to trust the hand of God. For example, He fed them with manna day by day. If God had not sent the day's manna, they would have starved in the wilderness. Every morning required confidence in God's provision. See how Moses warns them to remember the desert days when they get into the Promised Land?

Moses says that all this training and desert traveling was "so that in the end it may go well with you." Have you ever known anyone who achieved all they ever dreamed of, then lost it all through their own actions and choices? Moses tells the people that not only is God about to release the fullness of the promise into their lives, but He has prepared their hearts to live large in the abundance of His provision.

SMALL CHANGE

In some areas of your life, you have moved into the Promised Land and are living large. Look around and remember on purpose that God is the provider and sustainer. In some areas of your life, you are on a desert walk. When you feel the desert's heat, step back mentally and look for how God's provision is evident. Today, find one thing that you will thank God for instead of complaining about. Pray: "Do Your work, Refiner's Fire, that in the end it may go well for me."

DAY 7

Use your journal to think through and record your progress.

Have you started paying attention to longings toward God that are His invitation into deeper intimacy? How are you responding? Have you asked Him to breathe life into you?

Do you have a specific need or lack in your life right now? Can you embrace that need as God highlighting where He wants to work in your life? What are your thoughts and feelings about this today?

What step-by-step small obediences have you paid close attention to? How is it transforming your attitude and outlook to give more weight to small moments of obedience?

Have you found an opportunity to notice someone who had previously been invisible to you? What have you experienced in seeing the small and insignificant?

Is there an area in your life where it seems God is not paying any attention to your plight? Have you accepted that God is doing work you can't observe? Stop and clarify for yourself that you know God is working even when you can't see it.

Is there some area of your life where you feel that you are just putting one foot in front of the other, seeming to make no progress? What new insight do you have about the importance of one step?

DAY **8**

*"Bethlehem Ephrathah, you are small among
the clans of Judah; One will come from you
to be ruler over Israel for Me.
His origin is from antiquity, from eternity"
(Micah 5:2 HCSB).*

The account of the Incarnation of Christ, when the King of kings shed His kingly grandeur and donned mere clay, is packed with small. The little village of Bethlehem was singled out and marked as the location for Messiah's birth—the opening act of redemption. Pretty big stuff.

The location was so important that God revealed it through His prophets generations in advance. Bethlehem was no accident. It was one of the key elements in the unfolding of events.

The coming of Christ into the world was heaven's sole occupation. Every act, every event, everything was moving toward that one grand moment. Can you imagine that even one single detail was left to chance?

If you have ever been part of planning and preparing for a momentous event, like a wedding, or a celebration, or a conference, then you know how the details become the focus. No detail is too small to consider and plan for. In fact, the details are what make the event.

Heaven planned every single tiny component of the birth of the Savior. The location was specific, not random. Though in the incarnation narrative it seems that Mary and Joseph found themselves in Bethlehem by chance, the big picture shows that Bethlehem was planned. When the One whose "origin is from antiquity, from eternity"(Micah 5:2) transitioned from heaven's throne to little planet Earth, Bethlehem was to be the portal for His appearing.

Big, big God directed the small details—each on its own seeming insignificant—to culminate in the Savior of mankind being born in little Bethlehem. I wrote in *Pursuing the Christ*:

> You used the pettiness and greed of Caesar Augustus, the Roman ruler whose vanity compelled him to register and number the people under his rule in order to assure him the full amount of taxes to his treasury. His demand that every Hebrew resident travel to the town of his heritage and register according to lineage put Mary and Joseph in Bethlehem on exactly the night You had arranged. You use even the tyranny of tyrants to accomplish Your plan in Your way and at Your time. You brought Mary to Bethlehem to register her openly as a descendant of King David, the line from which the

Messiah would come. To establish His genealogy on the legal record, You worked everything out according to Your design.

BIG SHOTS

Caesar Augustus was a big shot. In the estimation of the world, he was the one with the power. He could enforce his will on the people under his rule. He could call all the shots. He could disrupt lives with his demands. Big shot.

From heaven, he didn't look so big. He looked small and shallow. He thought he was big, but he was really very small. Dictating and demanding as if he ran the world, little Caesar found himself a tool in God's hands. His ruling had no lasting effect in history except that it moved all the players into place and situated everyone for the birth of Jesus.

Big shots plan their big shot plans and rule as big shots in their little worlds, but God is ruler over all. All the time. Heaven has a different measuring stick than earth.

Certainly no one on earth would have planned to have the King born in one of the smallest villages, from among one of the smallest nations, to one of its most insignificant couples. But the plan for small beginnings doesn't end there. When Mary and Joseph got to little Bethlehem, circumstances forced them into the lowliest accommodations possible for the majestic birth upon which all of history hinged. Careful planning and detailed direction from heaven arranged that the preeminent event would occur in a stable in Bethlehem.

God—the universe's only real Big Shot—calls all the shots. And when He is orchestrating and choreographing His perfect plan, He searches out small. Small is the new big.

HIDDEN BEGINNINGS

God has always been big on small beginnings. He has built it into the cadence of the universe. A tiny seed holds the blueprint of a towering tree. A small rock thrown into the water produces a ripple effect that multiplies the impact for miles. Every human being has his or her beginning in a seed too small to see with the human eye.

Nothing can become big without first being small. It is the immutable law that governs the created world.

Sometimes we are called to small, even perhaps humbling, moments of obedience. Obedience that calls on us to die to all pride and embrace the power of small. In the moment, it is hard to believe that God designed this or that it could be elevated in any way. We can't extrapolate from the small obedience what grand outcome it might have, but we can know by faith that every obedience matters. It might be grooming us, or giving us needed experience, or simply conquering flesh that is fed by pride. But it matters.

Observe the story of Ruth, told in the Book of Ruth. Ruth had several strikes against her. She was widowed. She was poor. She was a Moabite, unwelcome in her adopted land of Israel. She had the responsibility of providing for her mother-in-law, Naomi. In order to feed herself and Naomi, she was reduced to a humbling act of gathering leftover grain. As she submitted herself to this demeaning task, she found herself right smack-dab in the middle of God's call on her life.

> And Ruth the Moabitess said to Naomi, "Let me go to the fields and pick up the leftover grain behind anyone in whose eyes I find favor." Naomi said to her, "Go ahead, my daughter." So she went out and began to glean in the fields behind the harvesters. As it turned out, she found herself working in a field belonging to Boaz (Ruth 2:2–3).

Boaz, a wealthy and influential citizen, fell in love with Ruth the Moabite and married her. Boaz and Ruth bore a son named Obed, who was the father of Jesse, the father of King David, from whom Messiah is directly descended. In Matthew's genealogy of Jesus, only five women are mentioned by name. One of those women is Ruth.

God often uses those small obediences to situate us for the provision He has in place. He always uses those small obediences to polish our character, to strip away our layers of pride and misplaced focus. He never calls us to an act of obedience that does not have an essential purpose in His plan.

Everything we do, we can do in an attitude of obedience to the Lord. Paul writes: "Whatever you do, work at it with all your heart, as working for the Lord, not for men. . . . It is the Lord Christ you are serving" (Colossians 3:23–24). C. H. Spurgeon comments:

> This saying ennobles the weary routine of earthly employments, and sheds a halo around the most humble occupations. To wash feet may be servile, but to wash His feet is royal work. To unloose the shoe-latchet is poor employ, but to unloose the great Master's shoe is a princely privilege. The shop, the barn, the scullery, and the smithy become temples when men and women do all to the glory of God! Then "divine service" is not a thing of a few hours and a few places, but all life becomes holiness unto the Lord, and every place and thing, as consecrated as the tabernacle and its golden candlestick.

If we are performing humble tasks for no other purpose than to obey and serve the Lord, then all tasks are transformed. If a manger, hidden from the view of all but a few, can become the birthplace of the King, then nothing God calls us to is servile. Rather, it is a privilege and we are honored by the call.

SMALL CHANGE

Daily every one of us has tasks that seem menial. As you approach those tasks, do them with all your heart as unto the Lord. Offer them to the Lord as worship. As you do that lowly task, pray: "Receive my act of worship."

DAY 9

"Go in the strength you have"
(Judges 6:14).

In Judges 6, God comes to a young Israelite named Gideon during a time when Israel was being harassed and overrun by their enemies the Midianites. Gideon is cowering, hiding away, minding his own business, staying out of trouble's way when God interrupts his life and calls him, of all things, a mighty warrior. "The Lord is with you, mighty warrior." Gideon thinks perhaps he's heard wrong. When God calls him to rescue Israel, Gideon wants to make sure that God has not accidentally called the wrong name, so he explains: "'But Lord,' Gideon asked, 'how can I save Israel? My clan is the weakest in Manasseh, and I am the least in my family'" (Judges 6:15). Here's the sentence that got me. As Gideon carefully explains to God why he, Gideon, cannot possibly be the one for the job, God says to him: "Go in the strength you have and save Israel out of Midian's hand. Am I not sending you?" (Judges 6:14).

Small strength? Small faith? No problem. Whatever you have—surrendered for God's use—will do.

The story of Gideon advances the theme of smaller is better. In the end, Gideon wins a great victory. But the road to a big win was paved with a whole lot of small.

SMALLER AND SMALLER

The enemy had crossed into Israel and set up camp, as they had been doing for seven years. The Spirit of the Lord fell upon Gideon and this essentially weak, frightened man began to behave as if he were a mighty warrior. The story progresses and the unlikely leader, Gideon, sends a call throughout the land for men to join his army and rescue Israel from the Midianites.

There were 135,000 enemy soldiers, and Gideon's ragtag, hastily called, untrained army numbered about 32,000. Small in every way you can measure. As Gideon was perhaps mentally assessing his chances of prevailing with such a fighting force, maybe strategizing about how he might find more fighting men to even the odds, the Lord says to Gideon, "You have too many men for me to deliver Midian into their hands" (Judges 7:2). Gideon's thinking, "Not enough," at the same time that God is thinking, "Too many."

I'm reminded here of a silly riddle—the kind that comes on bubble gum wrappers. The riddle says, "What gets bigger the more you take away?" The answer is, "A hole." But I think we might ask the same question and find that the answer is, "Faith."

God needs to gut Gideon's resources. Wait! Isn't God supposed to give? What's this with the taking away? God is very clear about why He is downsizing the provision.

> "In order that Israel may not boast against me that her own strength has saved her, announce now to the people, 'Anyone who trembles with fear may turn back and leave Mount Gilead.' So twenty-two thousand men left, while ten thousand remained" (Judges 7:2–3).

God wants the resources scarce—small—so that no one will be confused about the source of the victory. Why do you think God's pattern is big victory, small provision? Big outcome, small beginning? I think it is because we too quickly take the credit, or ascribe the credit to the wrong source. God wants us to know that He is all we need. He's the Big to our small. Always. When all the supply for our need is evident, life does not require faith. But when we learn how to answer the big call with small resources, it's a recipe for flourishing faith.

GIDEON'S 10,000

Gideon's army had decreased from 32,000 to 10,000. That should be small enough, right?

> But the Lord said to Gideon, "There are still too many men. Take them down to the water, and I will sift them for you there. If I say, 'This one shall go with you,' he shall go; but if I say, 'This one shall not go with you,' he shall not go."
> So Gideon took the men down to the water. There the Lord told him, "Separate those who lap the water with their

tongues like a dog from those who kneel down to drink." Three hundred men lapped with their hands to their mouths. All the rest got down on their knees to drink.

The Lord said to Gideon, "With the three hundred men that lapped I will save you and give the Midianites into your hands. Let all the other men go, each to his own place." So Gideon sent the rest of the Israelites to their tents but kept the three hundred, who took over the provisions and trumpets of the others (Judges 7:4–8).

Gideon's 10,000 became 300. Supplies were being taken away, and faith was growing stronger. Funny how that works.

The old, small Gideon had become Gideon, the mighty warrior. The Gideon who had defined himself as too small and insignificant for the call had learned the power of a Big God. So, when the Lord gave him the battle plan—the puny little battle plan that entailed trumpets and empty jars and torches—he didn't bat an eye. He was ready to take on the whole enemy's army and pit his small against their big.

He returned to the camp of Israel and called out, "Get up! The Lord has given the Midianite camp into your hands." Dividing the three hundred men into three companies, he placed trumpets and empty jars in the hands of all of them, with torches inside.

"Watch me," he told them. "Follow my lead. When I get to the edge of the camp, do exactly as I do. When I and all who are with me blow our trumpets, then from all around the camp blow yours and shout, 'For the Lord and for Gideon'" (Judges 7:15–18).

The Gideon who once said, "I can't lead!" now said, "Follow my lead!"

THE STRENGTH YOU HAVE

When the Lord first called Gideon, His challenge was, "Go in the strength you have. Am I not sending you?" If I may paraphrase it:

"It doesn't matter that you're small. I'm big." That one step, undergirded and carried forward by the power of God, is all it takes.

When it seems that resources are diminishing, allow your faith to unfurl. Let God work things out His way. Don't panic. Don't fret. Trust that the strength you have is all you need.

SMALL CHANGE

Is there any area of your life where supply seems to be getting smaller? Or any area of your life where you feel that you are not good enough or strong enough to do what you are being called to do? Don't project. Just do the next thing. One step, in the strength you have. When confronted with your feeling of inadequacy, pray: "Here I go, in the strength I have."

DAY **10**

*"Here is a boy with five small barley loaves
and two small fish, but how far will they go
among so many?"
(John 6:9).*

You know this story. Jesus fed a multitude of people—perhaps 10,000 when women and children were taken into account—with five small barley loaves and two small fish. I love the way Philip emphasizes "small" barley loaves and "small" fish. I assume he is emphasizing just how inadequate this provision is. I'm glad he was so specific in his description because now we will all be treated to a front row seat from which to observe the power of small in action.

Apparently, this was a spontaneous gathering. No one thought to bring food. They must not have considered the possibility that they would be there so long. They are likely to be traveling to Jerusalem for Passover. As we combine the accounts from all four Gospels, we get the idea that the crowd had been there all day and now it was late afternoon or evening. Jesus had been teaching them and healing those who needed it. Matthew, Mark, and Luke all report that the disciples came to Jesus and suggested that He send the crowd away to buy themselves something to eat. Imagine their surprise when Jesus said, "You give them something to eat" (Mark 6:38; Luke 9:13).

John reports something that none of the other gospels do. He tells about a conversation between Jesus and Philip. Maybe John overheard it. Maybe Philip told John about it later. Jesus says to Philip, "Where shall we buy bread for these people to eat?" I'm guessing Philip was a fixer. He analyzed problems and came up with solutions. He looked at a problem from every angle and didn't give up until he found the fix. I'm guessing. Maybe that's why Jesus singled him out for the question. He knew Philip's mind had already run the numbers. Philip had possibly already said to the others, "Guys! We've got a problem. There is no way that we can feed all these people. The only solution is to send them away to solve their problem on their own."

So Jesus says to Philip, "So Philip, what did you come up with? What's your solution? Where shall we buy bread for all these people to eat? Tell Me the best idea you could imagine."

Philip was ready with the answer. He'd already calculated it. He said, if you will allow me to interpret Philip, "I've reached this conclusion: there's nothing we can do. Even if we had eight months' wages, we couldn't feed all these people. This is a problem that we lack the resources to solve.

The only answer is to send them away and let them find their own bread."

Then John tells us—with a wink—Jesus was just giving Philip a test. A pop quiz.

> "When Jesus looked up and saw a great crowd coming toward him, he said to Philip, 'Where shall we buy bread for these people to eat?' He asked this only to test him, for he already had in mind what he was going to do" (John 6:5–6).

He was just giving Philip a chance to set aside his natural inclinations and let faith rule. Jesus already knew what He was going to do. Before they called, He answered. He's always working according to a plan. He is never at a loss.

Some of this crowd has been following Jesus for three days (Matthew 15:32). On this day, Jesus and the disciples had been ministering to this huge, needy crowd all day long. Can you imagine how tired the disciples were? And hungry? That's the state of things when Jesus says, "You give them something to eat."

Jesus had many options for how He could supernaturally feed this crowd. We know He could have turned rocks into bread. When Satan had said to Jesus, "You could just turn this rock into bread," Jesus didn't say, "No, I can't." He said, "I can, but I won't." So we know He had that power. Or He could have called down manna from the sky. Or He could have ordered the ravens to bring bread. He could have walked down to the lake, opened a fish's mouth, and found enough money to buy bread for the whole crowd. The possibilities were endless. But He chose not to take any of those tacks. Instead, He proposes the most outrageous and ridiculous solution: "You give them bread." Are you kidding? The disciples are as bread-less as the crowd. Where are they going to get bread? Are you hearing echoes of "Go in the strength you have"?

The conversation was lopsided. The disciples were focused on what they didn't have, and Jesus was focused on what they did have. The gist of it was something like this: His disciples said, "We don't have enough food for these people." Jesus said, "Well, then, just what *do* you have? Go in the strength you have. Bring Me whatever you *do* have.

Don't tell Me what you *don't* have."

If Jesus had worked around them instead of through them, the disciples would not have been searching, and alert to every possibility. They would never have paid any attention to a little boy with a little lunch.

"Another of his disciples, Andrew, Simon Peter's brother, spoke up, 'Here is a boy with five small barley loaves and two small fish, but how far will they go among so many?'" (John 6:8). Andrew must feel silly bringing what he has to Jesus. It's less than a drop in a bucket. But Jesus says something like, "Just what I was looking for!" You see, the "enough" is not in what we bring Him; the "enough" is in Him. Jesus is teaching His disciples, "It's not what you have, it's who I AM that defines the situation." He could do it without you, but instead He chooses to do it through you. Why? Because His power is made perfect in your weakness. When His power operates out of your weakness, then there is no explanation left except: The power of Christ rests on you.

THE MULTIPLICATION FACTOR

WorldCrafts℠ is a ministry started by Woman's Missionary Union, Auxiliary to Southern Baptist Convention. Established in 1996, WorldCrafts began with just one artisan group, Thai Country Trim, in Bangkla, Thailand. Today they work with dozens of artisan groups to import and sell hundreds of fine, handcrafted items from more than 30 countries around the globe. And they still work with Thai Country Trim, helping them employ more and more women at risk of abuse and exploitation.

The small amount that these artisans earn provides them with resources and freedom that is denied them otherwise. WorldCrafts helps create viable employment for women and men in poverty. Women no longer need to turn to prostitution for their next meal. Parents can provide education and nutrition to their children. Men can use their artisanal skills to earn a fair and reliable income without leaving their families.

A small start has multiplied to offer hope to many. One person whose life is redirected through the small wages earned as a WorldCrafts artisan, impacts those in her orbit differently than she would have otherwise.

Each of those people interact differently because of her influence. The effect spreads and is diffused into lives through generations.

One artisan group has multiplied into many. One small idea, enacted in obedience, has impacted untold numbers of lives.

SMALL CHANGE

Today stay open to small provision that God has already made available to you. Perhaps something you have overlooked because it seemed insignificant. A friendship? An ability? A small amount of money? See what happens when you put your small into His big hands. When you notice the small provision, pray: "In Your hands."

DAY **11**

"His master replied,
'Well done, good and faithful servant!
You have been faithful with a few things;
I will put you in charge of many things.
Come and share your master's happiness!'"
(Matthew 25:21)

Jesus told a parable meant to illuminate the kingdom of heaven. He wanted to teach His disciples how to live well in the kingdom—by the rules that govern the spiritual aspects of their daily lives.

He told a story of a rich property owner who was going on a journey. In those days, travel was unpredictable and even dangerous. He could not give a certain time for his return, and might, in fact, not return at all. In preparation, the ruler called his most trusted servants and gave them responsibility for his finances. He gave one servant five talents of money, another two, and another one. The two servants with the most money entrusted to them invested that money so that when the master returned, they had grown and advanced his kingdom. The servant to whom he had entrusted one talent was so fearful of losing the small amount he had, buried it in the ground to keep it safe.

In this parable, the master states clearly a kingdom principle: When the master wants to put the servant in charge of many things, he first puts him in charge of a few things. Training in the small things is where the seed of big things can be found.

Only when the Lord has taught you to do the small, behind-the-scenes, unnoticed work with integrity and joy can He entrust you with the bigger things. The key is to learn to do the work God calls you to for love of Him only. "I prefer the monotony of obscure sacrifice to all ecstasies. To pick up a pin for love can convert a soul," says Theresa de Lisieux.

I started what would become the ministry I have today teaching a Sunday School class of college women while I was a college student. I jumped at every opportunity to teach the Word, to small groups and individuals. The size of the group didn't matter to me at all and I had as my only objective to pour out what God had poured into me. As the Lord has slowly grown my ministry over the years, He has always kept me focused on where He had me, not where I thought I should be.

I remember very early in my ministry when I was young and untried. I was invited to speak at an event and anticipated a good attendance. When I arrived, the attendance was very low. I was exhausted and discouraged. I went to a room to prepare, thinking that I would just give the message I had outlined and get back home as soon as I could.

The Lord spoke so clearly to me in that moment. "You speak to these few women as if they were thousands. You give full measure, pressed down, shaken together, running over. The mark of a servant who serves Me out of love is that she will be faithful in the small things as if they were large." I heard that so clearly. It changed my attitude forever. That night I gave all I had to those women God had brought and I saw the big power of God move. Years later I was still hearing from women who were there and saw God move in might and change lives. I saw what God could do when my pride was out of His way, and nothing else would ever satisfy me again. Large crowds? I don't care. Large power? I can't live without it.

THE ONE-TALENT SERVANT

It seems to me that the unfaithful servant suffered from a skewed view of his master. He seemed to think that his master was testing him to see if he failed, rather than knowing that his master was training him in the power of small. What motivated him was fear of his master's displeasure instead of anticipation of his master's delight.

He thought that putting him in charge of something small was a slight, perhaps. He didn't recognize that it was an honor. We often think we're ready for something bigger than we are. Even when we have the skills or ability for something bigger, if we have pride and a feeling of ownership, we're not ready. Trust the Lord's timing in your promotion. Tell God right now, "I will stay right here, being faithful in the small, until I have been fully trained—until You entrust me with more."

FAITHFUL IN THE SMALL

Jan was a single mother who worked several jobs, one as custodial staff at a television studio. As she swept the floor and cleaned the bathrooms and wiped up the messes, she dreamed of being a television news anchor, or some other television personality because she knew what influence could be exerted. Jan was a devoted Christ follower and had a burning desire to bring others to Christ and to influence the culture. She struggled with her menial tasks, asking the Lord, "Why don't You put me where I can do some good for You?" Jan was bright, articulate, and even held a college degree, but year after year the doors to something bigger remained closed to her. She worked hard and was responsible, but she still chafed at what she thought of as less than what she could do.

One evening as she worked and argued with the Lord about the direction of her life, the Lord seemed to speak directly to her the words from Matthew: "Jan, be faithful in the small things. Accept the life I design for you. Find the things about this job that you can be grateful for. What you do, do as if You were doing it for Me." She began to look for every good aspect of her job. She had a lot of time to pray, she realized. The very thing she disliked about her job was the thing that left her free to be a vibrant intercessor. So she began to pray for each person whose office she was cleaning. She prayed as she walked the halls. She let each task be a direction for prayer.

One evening, as she had embarked on her new prayer mission, a producer was working late and Jan found herself in a personal conversation with the other woman. They talked about children and weather and all those things people talk about. They developed a friendship of sorts and the day came when Jan was able to lead her friend to the Lord. Jan saw her friend grow in Christ and begin to exercise the influence at the station Jan had started out wishing she could exert. Jan took great joy in knowing that because she had been faithful in the small things, the Lord allowed her to influence for Him as she had so desired.

Years have passed and Jan's children are grown, she is remarried, and has a responsible job that allows her to influence those in her sphere. She has never forgotten the lessons of the early days and says she lives, not for the next promotion or raise, but for the words of the Master: "Well done, good and faithful servant!"

SMALL CHANGE

Focus on the small tasks and be faithful in those. Every obedience matters. Take time to be fully present in the small events and responsibilities, embracing them as a way to love the Lord with all your heart, mind, and soul. As you engage in a small task, pray: "I pray that You can find me faithful."

DAY **12**

"If I just touch his clothes, I will be healed"
(Mark 5:28).

In the kingdom, no individual is small. No one gets lost in the crowd. One person, even one society has labeled worthless or impure, looms large in the Father's sight. The power of one small, helpless, unspoken plea.

In Mark 5:21–43, tucked into the gospel, wedged into the story of a high-profile healing, we find the story of a nameless woman who suffered from an undiagnosed illness.

We only have a snapshot of her. She appears on the scene briefly. We know one fact about her: she had been hemorrhaging for 12 years. Because of the ritual impurity her condition entailed, we know that for 12 years, no one has touched her. If a man had brushed up against her, he would have been made unclean because of her impurity. Imagine the times over the last 12 years that she had accidentally defiled a man. Imagine her humiliation and shame as the man scolded her and demeaned her. He would have had to rush home, tear off his defiled clothes, and cleanse himself in elaborate ceremony. It was very inconvenient to be touched by this impure one. Surely she had learned to hide herself even in crowds. Surely she had learned to gather her garments in closely, to cover her face, to become invisible.

Before we look at her story, notice how her story is framed. The framing of a picture brings out the details, focuses the eye. Look how her story is framed: it is framed by the story of Jairus.

Jairus, a leader in the synagogue—an important man, a man of influence—burst through the crowd that mobbed Jesus and, tossing aside all pride and dignity, threw himself at Jesus' feet. No doubt the crowd parted for such an esteemed man as Jairus. "Look! Here comes Jairus! Make a way for Jairus!" they might have said. No doubt they stared as he humbled himself and begged the Teacher, "My little daughter is dying. Please come and put your hands on her so that she will be healed and live" (Mark 5:23). Jairus was a daddy, and his little daughter was dying.

If you're a daddy, and your little daughter is dying, then no price is too high, no sacrifice too great. You'll do anything. You'll forget all your pride and position. You'll ignore every other duty.

If you're a daddy, and your little daughter is dying.

The crowd followed as Jesus headed for Jairus' house. They were not a quiet, sedate crowd. They were calling His name and reaching out to grab hold of Him; talking and shouting and clamoring for His attention. As they moved in the direction of Jairus' little daughter, I imagine that the crowd grew as the word went out, "Jairus' little daughter is dying! Rabbi Jesus is going to her! Come along!"

A woman stood on the fringes, watching. Alone. *Unclean.* Her uncleanness might rub off on anyone she came in contact with and that person would be forced to go through a time-consuming cleansing ritual to wash away her touch.

She had learned to be careful in public, avoiding brushing up against another person. But a thought kept worming its way into her imagination. "If I could just touch the hem of His garment, I would be made well." The thought grew stronger until, in a moment of reckless hope, she began to work her way through the crowd. The crowd didn't part for her as it had for Jairus. She prayed not to be noticed because to be noticed was to be rejected and humiliated.

Suddenly she was close enough to reach out and touch His hem and she was flooded with His power. Her touch didn't make Him unclean; instead His touch made her clean. She felt the cleansing, healing power of His touch transform her from death to life. Joy! Celebration!

Then, to her dismay, He stopped dead in His tracks. Brought the whole crowd to a screeching halt. "Who touched Me?" He demanded. She tried to hide, tried to disappear into the crowd, but He wouldn't stop asking, "Who touched Me?"

The crowd and the disciples were agitated. Why would He stop? He was on His way to do an important job. Didn't He remember Jairus' agonized cry: "Jesus, my little daughter's dying!"

There had been no daddy to part the crowds for the woman with the issue of blood; no daddy to cry out on her behalf; no daddy whose heart was breaking for her pain.

Or was there?

When at last, trembling in fear, she confessed that it was she who had touched Him, He looked into her eyes and said, "Daughter!"

Maybe, then, it wasn't just her touch that stopped Jesus in His tracks. Maybe it wasn't just her touch that caught His attention. Maybe it was the voice of her Daddy whispering, "Jesus, My little daughter's dying."

She had braced herself for the scorn she knew was coming. And found instead that He looked her in the eyes and called her by a new name: "Daughter, your faith has healed you. Go in peace and be freed from your suffering" (Mark 5:34).

Jesus was not satisfied just to heal her body. He wanted to heal her soul. When the healing flooded her body, she had what she desired from Him. But He did not have what He desired from her. He longed to bring her into His presence where He could shower her with love. He wanted to make her whole. He wanted her to know she had a Daddy.

LOST IN THE CROWD?

Do you ever feel lost in the crowd? Overlooked? Maybe even judged? You might believe that if anyone could see through your carefully crafted disguise—the veil you pull over the real you—he or she would call you unclean. Do you keep your true self hidden behind actions and lifestyle meant to protect you from scrutiny?

Today I had an email from my friend, author Barbara Wilson. She was speaking at the United Nations about women's issues. She has an amazing ministry and message about the effects of promiscuity on women and writes and teaches about healing from your sexual past. She travels globally working on behalf of women caught in situations that keep them in bondage.

How did it all begin? From a sexual trauma in her early teen years, Barbara acted out her hurt in hurtful ways. Her search for love led her in directions she later regretted and felt deeply ashamed of. Maturity brought redirection and she married and had four beautiful children. She lived a life that, to all appearance, seemed flawless. But, here is how she describes it:

> For 25 years I spent all my energy on redeeming, hiding, justifying and forgetting my past. Not only did it drain and stagnate me emotionally, physically and spiritually, but it negatively impacted all my relationships—with my friends, my husband, my children and my God.

Until God healed her and set her free.

She relates her turning point to the woman with the issue of blood. God was calling her to be public about her shame and His healing. She had been hiding herself all these years, right out in the middle of the crowd. What would all her friends and loved ones think when they realized she was unclean? But she made her story public where Jesus could use it for His purposes, and books and teaching and ministry that might have been forever veiled now flow freely.

A moment of radical obedience. One step. From that one yes to the voice of God, Barbara's voice has spread across the globe because she stepped out of her hiding place and told the story of her healing.

The Scripture says that we can live unveiled. "And we, who with unveiled faces all reflect the Lord's glory, are being transformed into his likeness with ever-increasing glory, which comes from the Lord, who is the Spirit" (2 Corinthians 3:18). We can live out loud and on display because we are reflections of the Lord's glory. That's how people see the reality of Christ in the world—through us living authentically and transparently.

Like the woman in Mark's story, you have been flooded with the presence of Jesus. Your shame has been removed. He can call you front and center in front of the whole crowd and say, "Your faith has made you whole."

SMALL CHANGE

Today be intentionally aware of the Father's tender mercies and loving kindness toward you. Let yourself enjoy His attention. Revel in the fact that you are not a face in the crowd to Him, but rather you are His dearly loved son or daughter. As you notice habits and responses that you have developed to hide yourself, deliberately step out of hiding. At these moments, pray: "Here I am."

DAY **13**

"If you have faith as small as a mustard seed,
you can say to this mulberry tree,
'Be uprooted and planted in the sea,'
and it will obey you"
(Luke 17:6).

Jesus used the metaphor of a mustard seed to provide some context for the power of faith. Even the smallest faith is so powerful that it can accomplish unimaginable things. Faith is such a powerful force that a little goes a long way. We might think that big feats require big faith, but not so. Enough faith to turn to Jesus is enough faith.

Look at an incident when Jesus identified "little faith."

> Then he got into the boat and his disciples followed him. Without warning, a furious storm came up on the lake, so that the waves swept over the boat. But Jesus was sleeping. The disciples went and woke him, saying, "Lord, save us! We're going to drown!"
>
> He replied, "You of little faith, why are you so afraid?" Then he got up and rebuked the winds and the waves, and it was completely calm.
>
> The men were amazed and asked, "What kind of man is this? Even the winds and the waves obey him!" (Matthew 8:23–27).

The disciples had watched Jesus perform miracles of healing that had to have rocked their world. He had just finished healing two infamous demoniacs so that they sat clothed and in their right minds. The disciples didn't suffer from lack of evidence that Jesus had the power of heaven to change the circumstances of earth. They were, I'm sure, trying to grasp it. As much as they experienced the power of God, Jesus still took them by surprise, and would continue to do so. Easy for us to feel superior, but I don't think Jesus was scolding. I think He was saying, "Congratulations! You had a little faith!"

We tend to "hear" the gospel accounts as if Jesus is always harsh and disappointed. Do you think He really expected His disciples' faith to be commensurate with His? Did He really think they should already know what He was about to teach them?

They had been overtaken by a furious storm. Not a little storm, or a medium-sized storm, but a furious storm. Jesus was very soundly asleep. They knew enough to know that their lives depended on Jesus.

They didn't say, "What good would it do to wake Jesus? He doesn't know anything about storms." That's all the faith it takes. Just to know to turn to Jesus is enough faith to release all His power on your behalf.

THE SIZE OF A MUSTARD SEED

In using the size of a mustard seed as the description, Jesus was using a typical Hebrew device for saying that something is as small as possible. A mustard seed was almost invisible to the naked eye, it was so small. Jesus was clearly setting up a parable about the power of small.

A seed is the embodiment of everything a plant or tree can become. All encased in the seed. Jesus used the idea of a mustard seed another time to talk about the way the kingdom develops.

> "What shall we say the kingdom of God is like, or what parable shall we use to describe it? It is like a mustard seed, which is the smallest seed you plant in the ground. Yet when planted, it grows and becomes the largest of all garden plants, with such big branches that the birds of the air can perch in its shade" (Mark 4:30–32).

THE MUSTARD SEED,
JESUS HAS ALREADY SAID, IS FAITH.

Though it is the sole keeper of the possibilities for any given plant, it is unimaginably small. The contrast of the beginning—the seed—and the full grown plant almost defies belief. Jesus points out that it is the smallest seed that grows the largest plant. Is there a clearer description of the power of small?

A seed must be planted before its potential can be realized. Until it is planted, it is a curiosity, a possibility. But once it finds good ground, it starts to send out roots and then to send up shoots. It grows progressively and its growth starts underground and out of sight.

Like faith. Faith grows by planting it and letting it put down roots. Faith has to have time to mature. It has to be deliberately sown into the ground. It doesn't have to be big, it just has to be put to use.

FAITH WORKS

Faith is acting in response to God's voice. It means risking everything on the conviction that God knows what He's talking about. For example, suppose you find that someone has deliberately done you harm. Maybe they have gossiped about you or denigrated your reputation. In some sense, that person has decided to become your "enemy." You want to get even. You want to retaliate. But, what does God tell you to do? He says to love your enemy and pray for anyone who despitefully uses you. Faith says, "I'm going to do what God clearly tells me to do, no matter how much I think my way would work out better for me." Every time you pray God's blessings on your enemy, in spite of how you feel, you are planting faith. Or, let's say that your finances are on shaky ground. You are concerned about being able to meet your needs. You feel pulled into worry and panic, showing impatience with those around you and spiraling into depression and fear. What does God tell you to do? Seek His kingdom, then everything else will be added. He doesn't mean not to work or to plan and be responsible, but He does mean that allowing anxiety to drive you and fear to hold you captive is counterproductive. When those emotions start pulling you under like the undertow in the ocean, break free by turning your heart and mind back to the faithfulness of God.

When you exert your faith by choosing to do what God says to do instead of what your emotions tell you, then you are planting your little faith. Leave it in the soil. Let it develop a strong root system. Don't dig it up to see how it's doing. It will take its natural course and, from the mustard-seed-sized faith will grow the largest tree in the garden. It will grow so big that it will provide shade and protection for others. Small holds the blueprint for large. Enact the small obedience in the power of your small faith and the large will result.

THE FRUIT OF FAITH

In October 1810, a 20-year-old girl in the quiet New England town of Bradford wrote the following words in her journal:

"If nothing in providence appears to prevent, I must spend my days in a heathen land. I am a creature of God, and he has undoubted right to do with me as seems good in his sight. . . . He has my heart in his hands, and when I am called to face danger, to pass through scenes of terror and distress, he can inspire me with fortitude, and enable me to trust in him. Jesus is faithful; his promises are precious. Were it not for these considerations, I should sink down with despair."

Ann Hasseltine had received a proposal of marriage from Adoniram Judson, who was shortly to leave for Asia as one of America's first overseas missionaries. Thus commenced one of the great dramas of church history. Ann and Adoniram Judson were pioneer missionaries in what is now called Myanmar. They labored six years on the missions field before they saw their first convert. Ann learned the Burmese and Siamese languages, did translation work, taught Burmese girls, and managed her household and cared for her husband during his 18-month imprisonment. Their various illnesses, personal tragedies, the danger to their own lives, are incalculable.

When you look at Ann's earliest reflections, you see weak and trembling faith. Mustard-seed faith. But she planted it in the soil of her life and the mustard tree has outlived her. One more advancement of foreign missions, and specifically the Christians of Myanmar, is the result of her decision to risk everything on the promises of God.

SMALL CHANGE

What challenge confronts you right now? Big or small, it doesn't matter. What would it mean for you right now to plant your mustard-seed faith in the soil—the situation God has in your life right now? Settle in your heart that all the work will be invisible for some time. Choose faith. When you feel tempted to dig it up, or take it back, declare: "My mustard-seed faith is planted."

DAY **14**

In your journal record your responses.

Is there anything menial in your life that you have been able to redefine as significant because it is done in obedience? What difference has that made in your life and in the lives of those around you?

Is there any task in your life that you feel too small for? How has the call to "go in the strength you have" changed your outlook and your actions?

Do you feel lost in the crowd and unworthy in any area of your life? Do you recognize ways that you try to hide your inadequacies—things, attitudes, or habits that you use to disguise the real you?

How does it make you feel to know that Jesus has singled you out for healing and wholeness?

Are there any tasks that have been reframed for you as you focused on doing them for the Lord? What difference has that made?

Describe in detail your mustard-seed faith. Can you acknowledge that it is weak and wobbly, but plant it anyway? Describe what it means to you right now in your life to plant mustard-seed faith.

What small change has been most significant for you this week?

DAY **15**

"Do not be anxious about anything,
but in everything, by prayer and petition,
with thanksgiving, present your requests to God.
And the peace of God, which transcends all
understanding, will guard your hearts and
your minds in Christ Jesus"
(Philippians 4:6–7).

Every command God gives us is to set us free. Our human nature leans toward actions and attitudes that diminish us and weigh us down. God's commands set us free. "I run in the path of your commands, for you have set my heart free" (Psalm 119:32).

Obedience to His commandments is how we find the abundant life for which we are created. Living large is the outcome of small obedience by small obedience.

God instructs us to suffuse our lives with thanksgiving and marinate our hearts in praise. Notice how Paul phrases this command in his letter to the Philippians. He reminds them of this command as part of his reminder not to be anxious. So, he is not talking about the kind of praise and thanksgiving that seems in line with events. He is saying wrap everything in thanksgiving, especially when the situation would seem to call for anxiety and worry.

I believe this is the key to living victoriously. Other things seem to fall into place behind it. People who have learned the value of praise and thanksgiving are fortified and ready for whatever life brings. But you learn it in the small things. That's where you integrate it into your life so that it is your default mode. It's like learning a foreign language. You have to practice it and immerse yourself in it until it is so much a part of you that you even think in your new vocabulary of praise.

When praise and thanksgiving overrule anxiety, anger, and fear, we find ourselves living on a higher plane. My mother modeled this kind of thinking as far back as I can remember, so she trained us in it. Look for the good. No matter how bad, let your thoughts land and park on the good. Little by little you will be trained to see the good without having to look so hard for it. You will see God's hand and provision in everything in your day, and then your life. I'm not talking about living in denial. You can face reality head on because the kind of praise and thanksgiving God is calling you to is based on reality.

A person who has not learned to see the reality of God's provision in every circumstance will have an entirely different view of any situation than a person whose sights are set on the activity of God. Sometimes you will be accused of not facing facts. But you are seeing all the same facts, just from a different vantage point.

THANKFUL FOR AND THANKFUL IN

First, learn to be thankful for God's work that you can see. Nothing dramatic. Every good gift is from Him. Everything in your life, every person in your life, every provision in your life . . . just make your daily life a praise fest. You don't have to make it a big deal. In your thoughts, have a shorthand way of saying thank you. It becomes the attitude that defines your way of seeing things. Practice gratitude in the things you take for granted.

Transfer that to the people around you. Start expressing gratitude more often. Look for ways to say a word of praise. Make it specific, and not necessarily about something the person has done, but maybe just about who he or she is—something you admire about them. It helps you keep the positive aspects of that person as your focal point.

Stay alert to every excuse for praise and thanksgiving to God, and then to those around you. You will be cultivating a worshipful heart, and an optimistic point of view. Every day has good and bad. Every circumstance has both positive and negative. It makes as much sense to accentuate the positive as it does to zero in on the negative. So, why not?

In every inconvenience that your day brings, look for all the ways it is positive. It takes the sting out. Praise and thanksgiving work as a spiritual antioxidant, keeping bitterness or resentment from doing damage.

Once praise and thanksgiving have become your norm, then when life's big hurdles and hurts come along, you will respond to them from a whole different place. You will have fostered a heart of genuine praise and thanksgiving in the small things and when the big things come crashing in, you will know how to move from panic to praise because of much practice.

When the earthquake hits home, you will find faith at the fault line. When the epicenter is right under your feet, you will find that your feet are planted on a rock. When the big events seem to come out of nowhere and throw your whole life off balance, you will have been trained by all the small events when you learned to keep your eyes on the provision instead of the problem.

When those terrible times come in life, God is not calling you to be thankful for them, but in them. You will already have your eyes trained to see the provision that is everywhere. You will see how God has prepared you for this storm, even when you didn't recognize what He was doing. You will see how He makes provision in the midst, and how He sustains you during and after. You will know for sure that God is in control, no matter how chaotic things seem. You will find many things to be thankful for because before the big, there was a whole lot of small.

ROCK-SOLID FORTRESS

How often the Scriptures describe God as a fortress and a rock, repeating the theme for emphasis and letting it get a foothold in our lives. Nothing else is unshakable. Everything and everyone else might let you down, and probably will. You have to learn that God is your fortress, and He is always a strong shelter.

He alone is my rock and my salvation; he is my fortress, I will not be shaken (Psalm 62:6).

But the Lord has become my fortress, and my God the rock in whom I take refuge (Psalm 94:22).

In October of 2005, my husband was diagnosed with an advanced case of an aggressive brain cancer. I must confess I did not see that coming. But, God did. As I look back over the whole experience I can see how God made such provision when I didn't even know what He was doing and the events seemed random and insignificant. To me, the most precious provision God made was the year before our earthquake hit. Our youngest son went off to college and we had an empty nest. Wayne's office was in our home. I had an office away from home and had worked that way for many years . That's how I liked it—home and work separate. But Wayne kept mentioning that I could take one of our spare bedrooms as an office. I mentioned it to my assistant, who felt that she could easily do her job from her home also. So, I just up and did it. No real reason behind it. It just suited my fancy.

That year Wayne and I had such fun. Both our offices at home and all alone. We could stop and visit any time of the day, run off to a movie, eat what we wanted when we wanted, decide what television show to watch, laugh hysterically at our own lame jokes. We thought this was just the first of many such years. We thought we were in the beginning stages of this season of marriage. God knew differently.

After his diagnosis, when for both practical and emotional reasons I needed to be right by his side, but I also had to continue working, I was so grateful that my office was at our house. And after he passed away and I was absorbed in my grief, but still had to work, I was so glad that my office was in my home.

I know it seems insignificant, but it was significant to me. And it is one of the provisions I can see most clearly and can describe most easily. You'll know what I mean when I say that there were a myriad of amazing provisions that are indescribable.

Let me tell you another story. One of Wayne's good friends, Jim Smith, was driving a couple of hours to have a visit with Wayne in our home. At this time, Wayne was still alert and able to enjoy company. Jim stayed for some time to visit. That same evening, while Jim was there, another friend, Libby Comfort, got an idea that the choir should come to our house that night after choir practice and sing to Wayne. So, most of the choir from our church ended up in our living room, just singing to us. Jim told us that as he was driving toward our house, he was singing that old hymn that says:

There is never a day so dreary,
There is never a night so long,
But the soul that is trusting in Jesus
Will somewhere find a song.

Wonderful, wonderful Jesus,
In the heart He implanteth a song:
A song of deliverance, of courage, of strength,
In the heart He implanteth a song.

Jim had prayed, "Lord, let Wayne find a song." One of the many small ways that the Lord reassured us that His loving hand was on this big situation. I found, and continue to find, so many reasons to praise Him in the midst of the storm.

SMALL CHANGE

Today be diligent in thanksgiving and praise. Do it when it seems to fit the situation. Don't take anything for granted. And do it when it seems the most ridiculous response. When something goes wrong—big or little—stop and catalog every good thing, then thank God in advance for how He is working things out. Tell someone else about it. Make this your continual prayer: "Thank You."

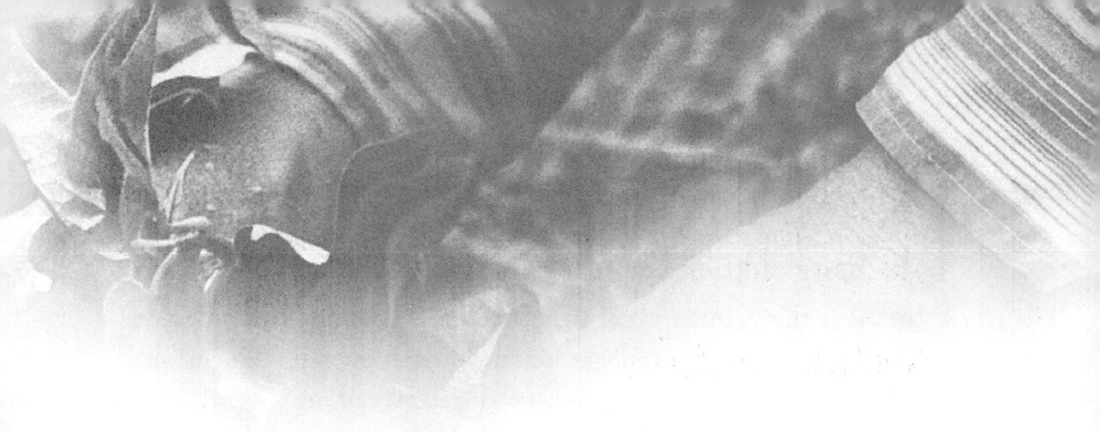

DAY **16**

"My command is this:
Love each other as I have loved you"
(John 15:12).

The eternally existent Word, who was with the Father from the beginning, became flesh. It changed the definition of words when the Word fleshed them out in real time on planet earth. The flat, one-dimensional words we thought we knew were now multidimensional, real-life, flesh-and-blood realities. It changed everything.

When God gave Moses the law and the Ten Commandments, the Word became language. It was revealing indeed. It revealed more of God than had ever been revealed before. When the Word became language, much was made apparent, but even more was kept hidden.

Here's where language falls short: I can only give a word the highest definition of that word that I have ever experienced. Take the word "love." When the word is language, it might mean one thing to me when I say it, and something different to you when you hear me say it. We both define it as we know it.

Now comes the Word made flesh. Love is no longer just language. Love is lived out in daily encounters with both friends and enemies. Love in the flesh. Forgive-them-even-while-they're-pounding-nails-in-your-flesh love. Die-for-them-while-they're-still-your-enemy love. Lay-down-your-life-for-them love. Altogether a new definition.

When the Word Made Flesh says, "Love each other as I have loved you," the command takes on a whole new complexion. Not love when I feel loving. Not love how I want to love. Not love in the most convenient way. It's the "as I have loved you" addendum that seals it.

It's a big call, but it is lived out in little moments.

GOD IS LOVE

Of course when the Word became flesh, the Word turned out to be love. Love sums it all up. Love to the uttermost, to the limit.

"My command is this: Love each other as I have loved you. Greater love has no one than this, that he lay down his life for his friends" (John 15:12–13).

Jesus expounded on His command to love as He loved by describing the highest expression of love: to lay down his life for his friends. There are many in our world who live their lives ready to lay down their physical lives for others. Our brave men and women in the armed forces, law enforcement officers, and others whose jobs bring them into physical danger. I am not such a person, and neither are most of us. For most of us, physically laying down our lives for others is a remote possibility. Yet, this command is to all of us.

Years ago the Lord began to explain to me how this worked in my life. Time and time again He calls me to lay down my life. Not my physical life, but my own self interests, my own schedule, my own comfort.

The love to which God calls us is specific and active. It nearly always means setting aside your own interests, even if only momentarily. Rarely is it convenient. It will almost never fit into your schedule where you have a break. It will mean lots of rearranging. Daily, there will be calls to love those around you like Christ loves you. Lay down your life and its self-focused vision. Actively loving those for whom you do feel love is inconvenient enough. But then, the call to love takes you further. Love your enemy.

Your enemy. The person who hurts you. You are called to that kind of love that forgives and reaches out even while the offense is still going on. Love that is active and pursuing relationship—not just tolerating politely.

Author Kent Hughes describes a situation in which big love grew out of little acts of kindness, deliberate acts of obedience.

> Several years ago one of my wife's friends took a missionary furlough with her husband and family after an unusually tiring stint of service. She had been looking forward to this time with great anticipation. For the first time she was going to have a place of her own, a new, large townhouse-styled apartment with a patio. She is very creative and made the patio the focus of her decoration.
>
> After a few months some new neighbors moved in. The word to describe them would be "coarse." There was loud music day and night along with a constant flow of obscenities. They urinated in the front yard in broad daylight. They totally disrupted her peace. She could see nothing good in them.

She asked the Lord to help her be more loving, but all she got back [from her neighbors] was disgust and rejection. The crisis came when she returned home to discover that her neighbors' children had sprayed orange paint all over her beautiful patio—the walls, the floors—everything! She was distraught and furious. She tried to pray but found herself crying out, "I cannot love them; I hate them!"

Knowing she had to deal with the sin in her heart, she began to converse with the Lord in her inner being, and a Scripture came to mind: "And beyond all these things put on love, which is the perfect bond of unity" (Colossians 3:14 NASB). In her heart she questioned, "Lord, how do I put on love?" The only way she could picture it was like putting on a coat. So that is what she determined to do—she chose to wrap herself in the love of God! As a result she began to experience a deeper life of Christ within her.

She made a list of what she would do if she really loved her exasperating neighbors, then did what she had listed. She baked cookies, she offered to babysit for free, she invited the mother over for coffee—and the most beautiful thing happened! She began to know and understand them. She began to see that they were living under tremendous pressures. She began to love her "enemies." She did good to them. She lent to them without expecting anything back.

The day came when they moved—and she wept! An unnatural, unconventional love had captured her heart—a supernatural love—the love of Jesus. (Kent Hughes, Luke, Volume One (Crossway, 1998), p. 229;/ http://www.preaching today. com/illustrations/2008/march/6033108.html)

LOVE'S SLAVE

Paul writes, "Christ's love compels us" (2 Corinthians 5:14). Paul is convinced that because Christ died for him, he is to live for Christ. According to Paul's reasoning, we "should no longer live for [ourselves], but for him who died for [us]" (2 Corinthians 5:15). Christ's love rules our lives.

"Live a life of love, just as Christ loved us and gave himself up for us as a fragrant offering and sacrifice to God" (Ephesians 5:2). A life of love is made up of small acts of love. Small ways every day that we set aside our own lives to become a fragrant offering to God. Love our friends, love our enemies, love people we don't know personally.

We were created to love—made in the image of God, who is love. The inconveniences of love move us into the abundant life. Instead of taking away from our lives, love adds to our lives.

Are there things you do for those you love, but you do them with irritation or resentment? Wife, do you pick up your husband's dirty socks, sighing and thinking irritably how many times you've asked him too pick up his own socks? Husband, do you run an errand for your wife, feeling resentful that she forgot to make time for her errand, so now you have to run it? Do you do the daily chores that your role demands for a family that you love, but as you do, you feel put upon because you are the only one who takes the time? Are you identifying with scenarios like these?

What if you instead did the routine acts, the blah, repetitive jobs, as if you were offering worship to the Lord? What if you said, "Thank You for giving me this avenue to love"? What if you decided to take joy in the acts?

Then what if you practice the same attitude regarding the loud neighbor, or the offensive co-worker, or the demanding employer? Can you imagine the stress that would be alleviated if you didn't have to be angry and resentful? You would have made a big change with small, in-the-moment decisions about living in love.

Love in the small things adds up to a life lived in love. Love as a grand idea or lofty concept boils down to a whole lot of small.

SMALL CHANGE

Choose one responsibility you resent. Make a decision to change how you think about it. As you fulfill that responsibility, say, "I offer my worship."

DAY **17**

"But I tell you:
Love your enemies and pray for
those who persecute you"
(Matthew 5:44).

When God calls us to love, He is not calling us to an emotion. He is calling us to a decision.

For most of us, those we might classify as enemies have done relatively little to really hurt us. And, I venture to guess that in most of those cases, the injury is to our pride. I'm sure there are some of you reading this who have an enemy who is truly working for your defeat. And, then there are a few who have real honest-to-goodness enemies. Whichever of these categories you fall into, whomever you think of as an enemy, hear the exorbitant command: love your enemy.

He is using the same word He uses to tell us to love each other, or love our neighbors. God's kind of love.

Let's talk enemies. If someone offends or hurts me, I can usually shake it off quickly. I'm always pretty sure that it was not their intent to hurt me. In fact, I'm fairly hard to offend. You'll really have to try hard. But, offend someone I love? You'll have me to tend with. Unless I let the Lord tame that flesh in me that wants to take on the offenders bare-knuckled and head-on. (Metaphorically speaking, of course. If I were speaking literally, I wouldn't be a very intimidating opponent.)

Even if you are not as thick-skinned as I am, you probably have a harder time forgiving the person who hurt your loved one than you have forgiving a person who hurt you. I think that's true of most of us. If so, you'll identify with Paula's experience.

When Paula's husband, Greg, was a young and inexperienced college graduate, his first job landed him in a growing young company and he got in on the ground floor. Years passed and his contributions to the business netted him a partnership. As the years passed, the difference between how Paula's husband wanted to conduct business and how his partners preferred to conduct business grew wider and caused rifts between them. Greg found every possible way to be cooperative without compromising because he so feared being let go and kicked out of the partnership. He felt that would be the worst thing that could happen to him, so he held on and held on. Finally the day came when his worst fear was realized. His partners voted to let him go. They did this in a way that made it obvious that they wanted to force him to leave the company. They put in place conditions and demands that should have guaranteed that he could not practice his profession without starting from scratch, and that seemed to be guaranteed to fail. They really were enemies, intent on hurting Greg.

The story is long, as God's stories often are. But the outcome was that Greg was protected from their unscrupulous conditions and set up his own business. Over the ensuing years, he has been more successful than in all the years he spent trying to maintain the fragile partnership.

Then the day came when Paula found herself ministering to a small group of which these ex-partners and their wives were a part. Though she had forgiven them from a distance years ago, this was a different story. How would this work? She knew the Lord had orchestrated it. She asked the Lord to let His love toward these individuals be what filled her heart. To her great surprise, at the first meeting when they first met, Paula reports that there was not one negative emotion surfaced. She felt completely free of anger.

I asked her what the secret was.

> From the first, I knew that the Lord was not going to let me keep my anger. I started from the first day to turn all that resentment and anger over to the Lord. At first, it didn't work too well. Then I had to be honest and say that it looked like the Lord took their side! He let them treat my husband like that. I was really just as mad at God as I was at them. Well, the Lord and I worked on through that. It took years, but I just never gave in to the anger. Year after year, it just got easier to let it go. I got in the habit of it, I guess. When I was going to be with them, I was afraid it wasn't real. I was afraid that when I had to be part of something with them I'd find out I was still mad. But what really happened was that I found out it was real after all.

One big moment of forgiveness grew out of a whole lot of small. The God kind of love looks like this:

> He does not treat us as our sins deserve or repay us according to our iniquities. For as high as the heavens are above the earth, so great is his love for those who fear him; as far as the east is from the west, so far has he removed our transgressions

from us. As a father has compassion on his children, so the Lord has compassion on those who fear him; for he knows how we are formed, he remembers that we are dust (Psalm 103:10–14).

WITH ALL MY HEART

Corrie Ten Boom has long been an inspiration, especially her story of forgiving an enemy. Corrie Ten Boom and her sister Betsie had been imprisoned by the Nazis and suffered greatly at their hands. Corrie's sister had died in Nazi imprisonment. She tells this story in her book *The Hiding Place*.

It was in a church in Munich that I saw him, a balding heavyset man in a gray overcoat, a brown felt hat clutched between his hands. People were filing out of the basement room where I had just spoken. It was 1947 and I had come from Holland to defeated Germany with the message that God forgives. . . .

And that's when I saw him, working his way forward against the others. One moment I saw the overcoat and the brown hat; the next, a blue uniform and a visored cap with its skull and crossbones. It came back with a rush: the huge room with its harsh overhead lights, the pathetic pile of dresses and shoes in the center of the floor, the shame of walking naked past this man. I could see my sister's frail form ahead of me, ribs sharp beneath the parchment skin. Betsie, how thin you were!

Betsie and I had been arrested for concealing Jews in our home during the Nazi occupation of Holland; this man had been a guard at Ravensbruck concentration camp where we were sent. . . .

"You mentioned Ravensbruck in your talk," he was saying. "I was a guard in there." No, he did not remember me.

"I had to do it—I knew that. The message that God forgives has a prior condition: that we forgive those who have injured us."

"But since that time," he went on, "I have become a

Christian. I know that God has forgiven me for the cruel things I did there, but I would like to hear it from your lips as well. Fraulein, . . ." his hand came out, "will you forgive me?"

And I stood there—I whose sins had every day to be forgiven—and could not. Betsie had died in that place—could he erase her slow terrible death simply for the asking?

It could not have been many seconds that he stood there, hand held out, but to me it seemed hours as I wrestled with the most difficult thing I had ever had to do.

For I had to do it—I knew that. The message that God forgives has a prior condition: that we forgive those who have injured us. "If you do not forgive men their trespasses," Jesus says, "neither will your Father in heaven forgive your trespasses."

And still I stood there with the coldness clutching my heart. But forgiveness is not an emotion—I knew that too. Forgiveness is an act of the will, and the will can function regardless of the temperature of the heart. "Jesus, help me!" I prayed silently. "I can lift my hand, I can do that much. You supply the feeling."

And so woodenly, mechanically, I thrust my hand into the one stretched out to me. And as I did, an incredible thing took place. The current started in my shoulder, raced down my arm, sprang into our joined hands. And then this healing warmth seemed to flood my whole being, bringing tears to my eyes.

"I forgive you, brother!" I cried. "With all my heart!"

For a long moment we grasped each other's hands, the former guard and the former prisoner. I had never known God's love so intensely as I did then.

I know this story has been told many times, but I want you to particularly take note of this sentence: "I can lift my hand. I can do that much." God will meet you with all His power and love when you take one step, feelings aside.

Pastor Robert Russell, in his sermon entitled "Releasing Resentment," tells this story of the power of forgiveness to transform a heart from anger and bitterness to loving ministry. The change is in the one forgiving. The call to forgive is out of mercy.

> When I was at the Eddyville State Penitentiary several weeks ago, I learned about Paul Stevens. Paul Stevens's daughter was stabbed to death by a neighbor in Evansville, Indiana, years ago. Paul Stevens spent nearly a decade tortured by the memory of his daughter's killer.
>
> A year later, the memories proved so hard to bear that Stevens moved his family from Evansville to a new home near Dawson Springs, Kentucky. His daughter's killer was released after seven years behind bars. Steven's hatred twisted his psyche. "At that time I wanted to see that man dead," Stevens said.
>
> In 1978, nine years after the murder, Stevens tried something radical. At a religious retreat, he finally grasped that his hate couldn't restore his daughter. He vowed to overcome the tragedy and devote his time to working with violent criminals. Since that time, Stevens has spent two days each week working as a counselor and lay minister at a maximum security prison. He has come to call some of the 29 prisoners on death row his friends.
>
> I met one of those prisoners who said he could never have been led to Christ except by this man who had such compassionate understanding. Stevens said treating violent criminals as human beings has helped him lose his hatred and made him a happier person. (Preachingtoday.com)

PRAY FOR THOSE WHO HURT YOU

A ssume that if God allows someone to bring pain into your life, He is highlighting that person for you to make him or her a prayer project. That's what He says to do about enemies. Pray for them.

We are inclined to pray that God will convict them of the terrible wrong they have done, or will reprimand them, or correct them. But we are to pray that God will bless them. Ouch! It is a nail hammered into our flesh.

I wrote this one day in my prayer journal years and years ago. In 1995 to be exact. It seemed to me the Lord was speaking this to me about forgiving an enemy:

> Deal the final death blow to the stubborn flesh that refuses to die. Don't hesitate because your emotions are not aligned with My purpose. Only I can change your heart, so don't try to do My job. Pray for the one who wronged you. Pray blessings and abundance for the one you are in the process of forgiving. Pour your anger and hurt out to Me, but pour My mercy out to your offender. I promise to give you opportunities to lift up and promote your offender. Do it, and keep on doing it, and soon you will be as you should be—all glorious within.

I love the way Thomas John Carlisle expresses it in his poem "Captured":

> Ensnared in our revenge
> we die until
> we claim the privilege
> of sharing His
> unerring mercy (You! Jonah!)

SMALL CHANGE

When someone who might be classified your enemy comes to mind, instead of spending your thoughts and time sucked into the vortex of anger, make a decision to pray blessings and abundance on that very one.

DAY **18**

"The tongue is a small part of the body, but it makes great boasts. Consider what a great forest is set on fire by a small spark. The tongue also is a fire, a world of evil among the parts of the body. It corrupts the whole person, sets the whole course of his life on fire, and is itself set on fire by hell"
(James 3:5–6).

I don't think I have to convince you about the power words wield. When you think back to eventful moments in your life, there are likely words involved, either encouraging or discouraging. Those words had power. They perhaps changed your course. The tongue is a perfect illustration of the power of small. James makes the point that though the tongue is a small part of the body, it can set the course for a life. Words are amazing weapons or great healers.

Connie L Peters expresses this beautifully in her poem "Wounded by Words"

> Wounded by words—
> No gaping hole
> No blood
> No bruise—
> Only a deep unseen slash that pierces the soul.
>
> It is more painful than any physical laceration.
> It severs,
> Paralyzes.
> Aborts progress productivity, and joy,
> And sabotages a fulfilled life.
>
> Lord, heal me from this wound.
> Let me speak blessings and hope in return.
> . . .
> Let your Words have preeminence,
> For your words are truth—
> A cleansing wash,
> A healing balm.
>
> You speak life and healing,
> Hope and truth,
> Joy and peace.
> Let me be
> Healed by Words.
> (From *Wounded by Words*, p. 16)

Author Charlotte Hunt tells her moving story in her book *Damaged Goods*. She tells the story of words that wounded her and had so much impact in her life that they almost derailed her and nearly kept her from becoming the amazing and dynamic woman she is. Charlotte came from a difficult and abusive situation, but found a relationship with Jesus Christ that transformed her. Early in her Christian walk, she was struggling with her faith and the call she felt in her life. Her early life experiences had taught her to be guarded in her dealings with others, but she opened up to a pastor, sharing her doubts and conflicts. He told her that because of her background, God could never use her in the ways she believed He would. "God can never use you."

You and I know immediately that those are silly words. But Charlotte, young in her faith and deeply wounded, was cut deeply. She writes the following:

> I was distraught and felt useless. I did not make a conscious choice in putting my hand up to God and saying, "I will handle my life on my own terms," but I did make a decision to take control of my life. Especially after hearing the pastor's response, I believed my show of weakness and vulnerability was the problem. . . . I understood that I needed everything to change from that point forward. The change was easy. I simply willed myself to be the person I believed people and God desired. I became strong, focused, self-dependent, and relied on my intellect and ability to manipulate and guide my life." (*Damaged Goods*, p. 74)

Words have to be managed carefully. Once spoken, a word can't be unspoken. You can't inhale and pull it back in. Words take on a life of their own. All words are modeled after the Eternal Word: living, active, sharp. If you let words fly in the heat of the moment, someone will have to heal from their impact. You can say, "I'm so sorry! I didn't mean that!" but the word is out and it lives in the person to whom you spoke it. No wonder the Word of God is jam-packed with warnings about using words prudently.

Words have the power to tear down, but they also have the power to build up. God can empower our words so that one small word can have so much impact that it redirects the trajectory of your life. God's work in our lives can be so deep that it changes our words. After all, words come right from the heart. Changed heart, changed words. We can be so much in His presence that we naturally speak His words. Jesus once said of His words: "These words you hear are not my own; they belong to the Father who sent me" (John 14:24).

I've always been accused of being exactly like my dad. People say that we are alike in looks, in temperament, in personality, in the way we process information, and in how we communicate. My two sisters, when the three of us are together, will often react to some statement of mine by looking at each other, rolling their eyes, and saying in unison, "That's Daddy talking."

They mean that I am expressing my own thoughts, but that my own thoughts are exactly like my father's. If he were present, he'd have said exactly what I said. You might say I'm speaking my father's words.

The thought is further illuminated in the Book of Isaiah:

> The Sovereign Lord has given me an instructed tongue, to know the word that sustains the weary. He wakens me morning by morning, wakens my ear to listen like one being taught (Isaiah 50:4).

An instructed tongue. Not a wild, untamed tongue, or a go-its-own-way tongue. We can have a trained, disciplined, controlled tongue. He wants you to speak words taught you by the Spirit. (See 1 Corinthians 2:13) When you speak with an instructed tongue, what kind of power do your words have? They have the power to sustain the weary.

Words generated in my own wisdom can reach only as far as a person's intellect or feelings. Words that are taught by the Spirit reach deep into the person and touch the spirit: "Deep calls to deep" (Psalm 42:7). Spirit-generated words can touch the spirit because they are "expressing spiritual truths in spiritual words" (1 Corinthians 2:13). These words are spiritual words because they were born of the Spirit. Everything that is born of the Spirit is spirit.

How do you learn the words that lift up the weary? "He wakens me morning by morning, wakens my ear to listen like one being taught"

(Isaiah 50:4). You learn by listening; listening carefully, attentively, like a student soaking up every word his mentor speaks. Respond to the Father's initiative. He wakens you morning after morning and unstops your spiritual ears.

The Father wants to speak His healing, encouraging, strengthening, eternal, life-giving words through your mouth. He wants to instruct your tongue. When He sends His word out through you, He has already given that word an assignment. The astonishing power of His Word will accomplish what He desires and purposes. (Read Isaiah 55:10–11.)

As you live moment by moment in His power and presence, he will speak His present-tense word through you. "The lips of the righteous nourish many" (Proverbs 10:21). You will speak what you have heard from the Father. When you speak, it can be said of you, "That's her Father talking." Jill Briscoe writes in her devotions:

> Give my words wings, Lord.
> May they alight gently on the branches of men's minds
> bending them to the winds of Your will.
> May they fly high enough to touch the lofty, low enough to
> breathe the breath
> Of sweet encouragement upon the downcast soul.
> Give my words wings, Lord.
> May they fly swift and far,
> Winning the race with the words of the worldly wise, to the
> hearts of men.
> Give my words wings, Lord. See them now nesting-down at
> Thy feet.
> Silenced into ecstasy home at last.
>
> From *Wings* devotional for women by Jill Briscoe

THE CUMULATIVE POWER OF WORDS

Words, once spoken, live on. Those words you speak to your teenager, thinking they are going in one ear and out the other? They are landing and making themselves a home. The words you thought you could throw out in a huff and apologize for later? They've carved out a nook and settled in. The words of kindness and encouragement that seemed to be ignored? They are fertilizing dreams.

Make it your goal to speak into lives such a preponderance of uplifting, encouraging words that they will eventually tip the balance and move a life from discouragement to hope.

SMALL CHANGE

Look for every opportunity to speak a word that sustains the weary. Strangers, family, friends. Speak them or write them. Let the power of small loose in your world through your words. Pray: "Let me speak with an instructed tongue."

DAY **19**

"My times are in your hands"
(Psalm 31:15).

Our times are in His hands. The expanse and the extent of my life; the events and opportunities of my life; the design of my life—all in His hands. Time is a commodity that the Lord has given us to spend wisely. When we use time as God intends, we will see again the power of small.

I learned a little about the power of small in terms of time from the microwave. I don't seem to have a very reliable internal clock. I can get lost in my work and think an hour has passed, only to find that the day is nearly over. Or, I can feel that a task takes a long, long time, so I keep putting it off, later to realize that it took a few minutes.

As a new wife, I wanted to do a good job being a homemaker, but I'm not very skilled in things domestic. I confess that every housework task seemed to me to be a huge, time-consuming burden. I would want to have the house all clean and tidy when Wayne got home from work, but I would spend all day putting off the terrible looming tasks until the last minute. Finally, I noticed something. I would put something in the microwave for a few minutes and say to myself, "I'll just work at this task until the microwave beeps." To my great surprise, by the time the microwave beeped, I had completed a task with a few seconds to spare. Amazing!

It occurred to me that I had spent the whole day dreading some task that I could have done quickly, leaving me the day to do the work I love without the background noise of guilt. The day is made up of minutes, each minute carries in it the potential for accomplishment. Every minute counts. It moves you forward, or it moves you backward.

I now sometimes have more work to do than I can imagine being able to get done. I've learned that I can look at the pile of work and let it overwhelm me, or I can just start doing it. Take it a task at a time. Don't think beyond to the next task, just do what is in front of you to do. Years ago I wrote in my journal: "New motto: do the day." For years, that has been my daily refrain when I feel overwhelmed. Whatever the day brings, do that. Just that.

As I considered the power of small in regards to time managements I began to soak my mind in these two thoughts:

My times are in your hands (Psalm 31:15).

This is the day the Lord has made; let us rejoice and be glad in it (Psalm 118:24).

God has allotted me exactly the right amount of time to do what He has called me to do. Once I really accepted that as my reality, I was amazed to discover how much work could be accomplished when I just rested in knowing that all I have to do is do the next thing, then the next thing, and an astonishing amount of work would soon be finished. My times include times for rest, for relaxing and having fun, and my time is multiplied by making sure the priority is time alone with God.

INCONVENIENCES

I've never done well with a schedule. I prefer a list. I love marking things off of a list so much that I sometimes add something I've completed to my list just so I can mark it off. But, when my list has times on it, it really throws me off. I'm kind of a go-with-the-flow gal. A lot of numbers on my list ruin it.

You might be just the opposite. You might love structure and schedules. You might get the most out of your time when everything has a time on it. I know people like you.

It doesn't matter either way. Time is a valuable resource to be spent well. A little goes a long way. Whether you work from a list or a schedule or a running commentary in your head, your carefully laid plans will be interrupted.

Your times are in God's hands. Reassert that first thing every morning and any time through the day that someone else's need interrupts your flow. Unexpected things come up. It's OK. God is running the show. He knows exactly how much time you have and what work has to be finished when. Just do the day.

I wrote a poem called "The Inconveniences of Love." It goes like this:

If I open my heart to You
Then I have opened my heart to the world.

Disturbing thought.
The world may not be respectful
Of my schedule
Or the demands on my
Energy.
The world may clamor for my attention
At inconvenient times.

Are there ever intervals
When the world
Is not on Your heart?

Perhaps we could arrange to meet
Then—
Just the two of us.
(Jennifer Kennedy Dean © 1995)

Here's what I was learning when I wrote that satirical poem, emphasizing my feeling that my time should be my own: God can interrupt me whenever He wants to. If I'm walking with Him, then I'm in the middle of all kinds of messes. He never keeps things sterile, or waits for an opening in my schedule. So, we have to find that balance between using time wisely and hoarding time for our own comfort. Only the Holy Spirit knows where that line is. He will tell you. You can trust Him.

We also have to learn the miracle of multiplied and empowered time. I have been surprised by it many times. When God is our scheduler, time will not be lost. When some inconvenience of love wrecks my timetable, when I get back to it, I find my energy, creativity, and—somehow—my time multiplied. The power of small is validated when we see how much can come out of a small commitment of time.

PURPOSEFUL LIVING

The reason that time is such a valuable and precious commodity is that God has measured it out and has a purpose for it.

Who, then, is the man that fears the Lord? He will instruct him in the way chosen for him. He will spend his days in prosperity, and his descendants will inherit the land. The Lord confides in those who fear him; he makes his covenant known to them (Psalm 25:12–14).

There is a way appointed for you. God did not create a purpose for you, He created you for a purpose. "We are God's workmanship, created in Christ Jesus to do good works, which God prepared in advance for us to do" (Ephesians 2:10).

The Creator has placed into humans a craving for purpose and direction. This craving is meant to lead each person to the One who created him with a specific purpose in mind. A sense of purpose gives life meaning. It creates a joyful, expectant outlook. The keener the sense of calling or purpose, the more satisfied we feel. Your purpose, my purpose, was assigned to us before we were born on planet Earth. When we were nothing but a plan of God, our purpose was already assigned. The timing of our birth, the location of our home, the family into which God placed us, the experiences God allowed and the experiences He engineered—all have to do with a preassigned purpose. God put you on the earth when and where you could accomplish your purpose—find the way chosen for you.

"Before I formed you in the womb I knew you, before you were born I set you apart" (Jeremiah 1:5).

Your eyes saw my unformed substance. All the days ordained for me were written in your book before one of them came to be (Psalm 139:16).

"I am the Lord your God, who teaches you what is best for you, who directs you in the way you should go" (Isaiah 48:17).

Look at Jesus' sense of purpose and how it enabled Him to use His time wisely:

- *His sense of purpose gave Him wisdom in making decisions.* When the crowds were imploring Him to stay with them, Jesus said, "'I must preach the good news of the kingdom of God to the other towns also, because that is why I was sent'" (Luke 4:43).

- *His sense of purpose enabled Him to serve instead of demanding to be served.* "Jesus knew that the Father had put all things under his power, and that he had come from God, and was returning to God; so he got up from the meal, took off his outer clothing, and wrapped a towel around his waist. . . . He began to wash the disciples' feet" (John 13:3–5).

- *His sense of purpose sustained Him through the agonizing days of rejection, humiliation, torture, and death.* "'Now my heart is troubled, and what shall I say? "Father, save me from this hour"? No, it was for this very reason I came to this hour. Father, glorify yourself'" (John 12:27–28).

Jesus walked in the way chosen for Him, and He lived joyfully. In the continual search for meaning and direction, this truth emerges: Jesus called Himself the Way. When we find His way, we find our way.

Purposeful living gives time its value. You are not wandering around blindly. Rather, you are moving steadily in a forward direction. The time that God has designed for you is exactly right.

SMALL CHANGE

Start your day with the prayer: "My times are in Your hands." Be aware of spare minutes and find a way to use them purposefully. Enjoy the peaceful rest that comes after spending time wisely.

DAY **20**

*"As he looked up, Jesus saw the rich
putting their gifts into the temple treasury.
He also saw a poor widow put in two very small
copper coins. 'I tell you the truth,' he said, 'this poor
widow has put in more than all the others. All these
people gave their gifts out of their wealth; but she
out of her poverty put in all she had to live on'"
(Luke 21:1–4).*

Jesus, observing the comings and goings at the temple, had seen numerous displays of wealth as the pillars and leaders of the community dropped their offerings—many of them with great fanfare—into the treasury chests that sat in the temple's outer courtyard. It's said that a person might drop his offering from as high as he could reach so that it would make the loudest sound and attract the most attention.

Jesus didn't dismiss the gifts of the wealthy, but He did call attention to the small gift of a widow. In a setting where many were hoping to be noticed and admired, the widow quietly gave her gift, assuming it to be so paltry that it would not make any waves. She was not giving out of a desire to be admired, but out of love and obedience. That's what set her gift apart. That's what gave her gift its heft. The value of our monetary gifts to the kingdom is that it is a measure of our hearts.

In looking at the money we give to kingdom causes, we again see the power of small. The most important gift given that day was the smallest gift of all. She gave extravagantly. The amount of money given to support kingdom causes really doesn't matter. God can multiply it and use small amounts to accomplish big results. If the wealthiest person on earth were to give all he had to the work of the kingdom, it would be a small amount. God would make no more use of a gargantuan sum than He made of the widow's gift. What matters is what your financial gifts into the kingdom say about your priorities.

I know, it's an uncomfortable subject. Many would say that their finances are the hardest realm in which to trust and obey God. Bill White, pastor or outreach at Emmanuel Reformed Church in Paramount, California, tells the following story.

> Craig C. had been an alcoholic for more than a dozen years. He'd lost everything he had, including his wife and son, due to his selfishness and addiction. Things began to change after he gave his life to Christ, but he still fell regularly into his old habits. It didn't help that he'd lost his well-paying job and was clerking at a local grocery store that was well stocked with all his favorite drinks. After a few years of going back and forth

between Christ and the bottle, he finally cut the ties, and, out of obedience to Christ, quit his job.

With no income and hope only in Christ, he was in desperate condition. After an interview with a sheet metal company down the street from his new church, he cried out to God. "God, if you give me this job I will give you my first paycheck." Surprisingly, he got the job.

He clearly remembers the day when he got his first paycheck. Stacks of bills needed to be paid. Penniless but determined, he endorsed it over to the church and walked it to the church office without waiting for the Sunday offering. That was the moment, he says, that changed his life because now he understood what it meant to trust God.

As of today, Craig has been sober for 25 years, he's a manager at that sheet metal company, and he serves as an elder at his local church.

A friend of mine used to say, "I write my tithe and gift checks as soon as I get my paycheck before I get too attached to my money." Money can take possession of a heart in no time. Money is one of those things that sneaks up on you and owns you before you know what happened. I never cease to be surprised when I find out that someone who makes lots and lots and lots of money can be deeply in debt and living paycheck to paycheck. For most people, there's no such thing as enough money.

God makes a big deal over money given into the kingdom. He knows how easily we can come to love it and let it dictate our lives, influence our decisions, determine our emotional state. Money can become an idol faster than almost anything you can name. That's why God wants us to remember that it is all His.

Why do you think He chooses to finance His work and meet the needs of His children through the financial gifts of His people? Primarily, I think, He allows His people to give because that obedience releases His abundance. Luke 6:38 says, "Give, and it will be given to you. A good measure, pressed down, shaken together and running over, will be poured into your lap. For with the measure you use, it will be measured to you."

This concept is found throughout Scripture. Pay particular attention to His wonderful promise to provide for all our needs through His riches in Christ Jesus (Philippians 4:19). Look at the thoughts that lead up to that promise:

> I rejoice greatly in the Lord that at last you have renewed your concern for me. Indeed, you have been concerned, but you had no opportunity to show it. I am not saying this because I am in need, for I have learned to be content whatever the circumstances. I know what it is to be in need, and I know what it is to have plenty. I have learned the secret of being content in any and every situation, whether well fed or hungry, whether living in plenty or in want. I can do everything through him who gives me strength (Philippians 4:10–13).

The Philippians are not the source of Paul's supply. God is the source of his supply. Paul is not dependent upon the gifts of the Philippians; but they need an opportunity to show their commitment in tangible ways. Paul is looking to His Father for all of his needs.

> Yet it was good of you to share in my troubles. Moreover, as you Philippians know, in the early days of your acquaintance with the gospel, when I set out from Macedonia, not one church shared with me in the matter of giving and receiving, except you only; for even when I was in Thessalonica, you sent me aid again and again when I was in need. Not that I am looking for a gift, but I am looking for what may be credited to your account (Philippians 4:14–17).

Paul is doing the Philippians a favor by allowing them to give.

> I have received full payment and even more; I am amply supplied, now that I have received from Epaphroditus the gifts you sent. They are a fragrant offering, an acceptable sacrifice, pleasing to God (Philippians 4:18).

God sees our gifts as "a fragrant offering, an acceptable sacrifice, well-pleasing to God." Giving is worship.

And my God will meet all your needs according to his glorious riches in Christ Jesus (Philippians 4:19).

Giving activates the wonderful promise that God will supply all your needs.

To our God and Father be glory for ever and ever. Amen (Philippians 4:20).

THE ULTIMATE RESULT OF OUR GIVING IS THAT GOD IS GLORIFIED

We are the body of Christ. When I give, I am pouring out costly ointment, anointing the body of Jesus as an act of love and worship to Him. My prayer is that God will give you many opportunities to give—and give—and give some more, and that you will find an even fuller measure of His overflowing joy. As you engage in the spiritual discipline of giving, you are discovering that "where your treasure is, there your heart will be also" (Luke 12:34). When you invest your treasure in the kingdom, your heart will follow. That's why you give first, before you get too attached to your money.

SEEKING SMALL

It seems to be a pattern that God seeks out the least likely person to give. I think because He wants to open the flow of provision, and that is His appointed way. In 2 Kings 4:1–6, a story is recorded about God's provision for His prophet Elijah. Elijah, after besting the prophets of Baal in a showdown, and escaping the evil trap of Jezebel, had spent three years hiding out by a brook, where he drank from the brook and was fed by the ravens. "You will drink from the brook, and I have ordered the ravens to feed you there" (1 Kings 17:4). Notice that God had ordered the ravens to feed Elijah.

Eventually the brook dried up. God said, "Go at once to Zarephath of Sidon and stay there. I have commanded a widow in that place to supply you with food" (1 Kings 17:9). Previously, God had commanded the ravens to feed Elijah, and now He has commanded a certain widow to feed him. God had many ways that he could have fed and nourished Elijah. The ravens could still have fed him. Or, this was the same God who had made water gush from a rock and caused manna to appear every morning. He could still do that. But He wanted to provide for Elijah through a certain widow.

How was Elijah to know which widow? As it turned out, when he arrived at the town gate, a widow was there gathering wood. He asked her for some water, and as she was going to get water, Elijah added a request: "And a little bread?"

As the story unfolds, it is unmistakable that this is the very widow God has commanded to supply Elijah with food, but she doesn't know she has been commanded. When Elijah asks for the bread, she reveals her situation. She doesn't have any bread. All she has is a handful of flour and a little oil. Just enough to make her and her son a small meal so they can eat it and then lie down to die. She is at the end of her provision. There is no more and she sees no possible way to get more.

This is the widow God has commanded to feed Elijah. The one who was fresh out of food.

Elijah told her to ignore her lack of provision and act as if she had plenty. He told her to go make a small cake of bread for him from her almost empty supply and then make one for herself and her son. Sounds reasonable. She was almost out of food, so she should share that food with one more person. Stretch it further.

As soon as she obeyed the Lord, provision began. The jar of flour was not used up and the jug of oil did not run dry. Every time she needed four and oil, flour and oil were there.

Why did God command this destitute widow to give out of the little she had to provide for the Lord's prophet? So that she could obtain the blessing that giving brings. So that she could receive in the measure she gave. So that she could set in motion the kingdom law that releases the Lord's abundant and perfect provision in response to obedience.

Her small became large when she acknowledged with her actions that God was the owner of all she possessed. When she let go of all she had—small though it was—she received abundant life.

SMALL CHANGE

Give some money. You are not giving it to an institution or an organization or a person. You are giving it to God. As you give, pray: "Multiply this offering."

DAY **21**

Record your thoughts in your journal.

❧

How have you incorporated praise and thanksgiving into your life in all the small moments? What difference has it made in your outlook?

❧

What small acts of love have you performed this week? What burdensome responsibilities have you redefined as acts of loving worship? Describe your experience.

❧

How have you evaluated your use of time? Where and how do you need to improve?

❧

What ways has your schedule been interrupted this week and how did you respond? What did you learn from the interruption?

❧

Have you recognized ways that your money is an issue in your life? Has anything come to mind about where you should give money into the kingdom and loosen your attachment to money?

❧

How uncomfortable is it for you to consider the role of money in your spiritual walk? Why do you think that is?

❧

DAY **22**

*"So David triumphed over the Philistine with a
sling and a stone; without a sword in his hand
he struck down the Philistine and killed him"*
(1 Samuel 17:50).

We can hardly conclude a look at the power of small without including David and Goliath. The power of small is on display big time.

Saul was king of Israel. When Saul first comes on the scene as Samuel is looking for a king to anoint, Saul is described as "an impressive young man without equal among the Israelites—a head taller than any of the others" (1 Samuel 9:2). He looked the part. He just seemed like a guy who could the job.

Saul had proven that just because he was straight out of central casting—all kingly looking—didn't mean anything when it came down to doing the job. By the time of the famous Goliath incident, Saul had been rejected by God as king and his successor had been chosen.

David was God's choice to succeed Saul, and He was leading Samuel to His chosen. He sent Samuel to Jesse, father of David. But David was the baby of the family, and apparently the least impressive. When Samuel saw Jesse's son, Eliab, he thought something like, "This has to be the guy. Just look at him." But the Lord said,

> "Do not consider his appearance or his height, for I have rejected him. The Lord does not look at the things man looks at. Man looks at the outward appearance, but the Lord looks at the heart" (1 Samuel 16:7).

Seven of Jesse's sons were presented to Samuel for consideration, but God declined each. Jesse didn't even say, "Hey! Wait! I've got one more son." Apparently, Jesse thought that if these seven didn't pass muster, then baby son David certainly would not. Samuel had to ask Jesse if there was anybody else.

So he asked Jesse, "Are these all the sons you have?" "There is still the youngest," Jesse answered, "but he is tending the sheep." Samuel said, "Send for him; we will not sit down until he arrives" (1 Samuel 16:11).

The baby of the family. Though he would someday look the part, David didn't look the part that day. But Samuel secretly anointed him to be the successor of Saul.

The Lord worked out a way for David to be in training under Saul without Saul knowing. Saul was visited by an evil spirit and needed someone to play the harp to soothe him. He instructed his servants to find someone who plays well, and one of the servants found David. David entered the service of King Saul and King Saul liked him very much. David began to go back and forth between waiting on Saul and tending his father's sheep.

That's how things stood when Israel went to war with the Philistines. Enter Goliath. He was nearly nine feet tall. Remember the giants who had so intimidated the Hebrew spies all those years ago? Goliath was of that tribe. He had a helmet on his head, bronze armor that weighed as much as a grown man, his legs were covered in bronze and he had a bronze javelin on his back. On top of all that, he carried a spear shaft that was like a weaver's rod with an iron point that weighed 15 pounds. He was big and then he was covered in big and he carried a big weapon.

For 40 days, every morning and every night Goliath came out and mocked the Israelite army. Eighty times he shouted out his intimidating defiance and was met with fear and fleeing. On the 81st time, he got the surprise of his life.

When you are living with an awareness of the power of small, you will notice that some small, insignificant thing puts you where you need to be when you need to be there. In David's case, his father asked him to take food to his brothers on the front lines and David happened to arrive just as Goliath began his morning rant.

Israel's army had been frightened off every day for 40 days by Goliath's goading threats. They looked at his size and compared him to their own size. The biggest soldier of Israel was small in comparison. The Scripture says they were dismayed and terrified (1 Samuel 17:11). Shaking in their boots.

They were focused on his size. That's what did it for them. He was big and loud. When David first heard Goliath's taunts, his reaction was: "Who is this uncircumcised Philistine that he should defy the armies of the living God?" (1 Samuel 17:26). David didn't even mention Goliath's size. David was comparing Goliath to God and Goliath was not coming out the winner. In David's eyes, Goliath was puny.

Little David decided to take on the giant. Saul's response was: "You are only a boy, and he has been a fighting man from his youth" (1 Samuel 17:33). Saul took a look at Goliath, then took a look at David, and reached the only conclusion he knew how to reach. He looked at the empirical evidence and deduced: Big will win, small will lose.

But this monumental event had some precedents in David's life. David had been trained in the power of small.

> But David said to Saul, "Your servant has been keeping his father's sheep. When a lion or a bear came and carried off a sheep from the flock, I went after it, struck it and rescued the sheep from its mouth. When it turned on me, I seized it by its hair, struck it and killed it. Your servant has killed both the lion and the bear; this uncircumcised Philistine will be like one of them, because he has defied the armies of the living God. The Lord who delivered me from the paw of the lion and the paw of the bear will deliver me from the hand of this Philistine" (1 Samuel 17:34–36).

God had been training David for this encounter. His training came in the form of a whole lot of small. I'm sure in real time the bear and the lion had looked big, but now they seemed small. David had not been trained in battle, but he had been trained in the power of God.

To emphasize how small David was, the Scripture reports that Saul dressed David in his tunic and armor, but David couldn't walk around in them. They were too cumbersome and instead of helping him, they hindered him. When David stepped out to meet the giant, armored Goliath, he was the very picture of small. Goliath couldn't believe his eyes.

> He looked David over and saw that he was only a boy, ruddy and handsome, and he despised him. He said to David, "Am I a dog, that you come at me with sticks?" And the Philistine cursed David by his gods (1 Samuel 17:42–43).

Little David was undaunted. He ran right at Goliath, took a stone out of his shepherd's bag, slung it and killed Goliath. "So David triumphed over the Philistine with a sling and a stone; without a sword in his hand he struck down the Philistine and killed him" (1 Samuel 17:50).

Let's stand back from the story for a minute and watch it unfold from a distance. Goliath was big and loud and intimidating, but very likely it was all a cover. His size made him a big target. His armor kept him from being agile and light on his feet. The design of his helmet likely restricted his peripheral vision so that he had to completely turn his big helmeted head all the way around to follow the quick movements of David. His fearsome weapon was heavy and unwieldy and he had to get it balanced just right in order to throw it.

David, on the other hand, was small and nimble and unencumbered. David had seen how God could use the power of small to win big battles. He didn't try to fight the battle like someone else might have done it. He did it the way he had learned. And it worked.

When you look at the story that way, you see that everything that looked like strength was really weakness and everything that looked like weakness was really strength. What looked like a liability was an asset. When you acclimate to the power of small, you will recognize it working everywhere you look. When you're the "small" in the equation, you won't be intimidated and try to make someone else's battle gear fit you. You'll go in the strength you have because God is sending you.

ONE SMALL WOMAN, ONE SMALL ACT

In the 1950s the United States entered into a battle around the call for civil rights. Most historians date the beginning of the modern civil rights movement in the United States to December 1, 1955. That was the day when an unknown seamstress in Montgomery, Alabama, refused to give up her bus seat to a white passenger. This brave woman, Rosa Parks, was arrested and fined for violating a city ordinance, but her lonely act of defiance began a movement that ended legal segregation in America, and made her an inspiration to freedom-loving people everywhere. http://www.achievement.org/auto doc/page/par0bio-1 (Academy of Achievement achievement.org)

That famous courageous act created a ripple effect that continues to make a difference generations later. Our country is different because a woman faced the giant. A small act of bravery seeded a movement that rerouted our country's history.

SMALL CHANGE

Face a giant today. What have you held back about because you felt small in comparison to the challenge? Today, make a move or stand your ground in the strength you have.

DAY **23**

"The seventh time the servant reported,
'A cloud as small as a man's hand is rising from
the sea.' So Elijah said, 'Go and tell Ahab,
"Hitch up your chariot and go down
before the rain stops you"'"
(1 Kings 18:44).

When the servant saw a cloud "as small as a man's hand"—hardly worth mentioning—Elijah, whose inner eyes were trained on the spiritual realm, saw a mighty rain that would end a three-and-a-half-year drought. Elijah knew the power of small.

For three and a half years there had been a severe drought on the land. Elijah had announced the drought to big King Ahab, then Elijah—in obedience to the Lord's command—hid. He made the excursion to Zarephath and was fed by the widow whom God appointed as provision, as we read on Day 20. Then God gave Elijah the next step: "After a long time, in the third year, the word of the Lord came to Elijah: 'Go and present yourself to Ahab, and I will send rain on the land.' So Elijah went to present himself to Ahab" (1 Kings 18:1–2).

So often, God creates the conditions so that when He acts, He is the only explanation. He could have just sent the rain, but instead He invited Elijah into His work. He wanted Elijah to give Ahab the news before it happened. Elijah is small and defenseless and Ahab is big and powerful. Ahab doesn't like Elijah at all.

To freeze-frame Elijah's small, God arranged a showdown between Elijah and the prophets of Baal. Here is Elijah's situation: "Then Elijah said to them, 'I am the only one of the Lord's prophets left, but Baal has four hundred and fifty prophets'" (1 Kings 18:22). Ready to watch the power of small?

All the prophets of Baal—450 of them—and all the prophets of Asherah—400 of them—gathered at Mt Carmel. Lone Elijah was looking pretty small right about then. As agreed, they prepared bulls for sacrifice and placed them on the altar but didn't light the fire.

The big guys went first. They put on a big, loud, long show.

> So they took the bull given them and prepared it. Then they called on the name of Baal from morning till noon. "O Baal, answer us!" they shouted. But there was no response; no one answered. And they danced around the altar they had made.

At noon Elijah began to taunt them. "Shout louder!" he said. "Surely he is a god! Perhaps he is deep in thought, or busy, or traveling. Maybe he is sleeping and must be awakened."

So they shouted louder and slashed themselves with swords and spears, as was their custom, until their blood flowed.

Midday passed, and they continued their frantic prophesying until the time for the evening sacrifice. But there was no response, no one answered, no one paid attention (1 Kings 18:26–29).

Then came Elijah's turn. He dug a trench around the altar, placed the offering on the altar, drenched the altar and the wood until the water ran down into the trench. Then he prayed. Contrast Elijah's prayer with the prayer of Baal's prophets.

At the time of sacrifice, the prophet Elijah stepped forward and prayed: "O Lord, God of Abraham, Isaac and Israel, let it be known today that you are God in Israel and that I am your servant and have done all these things at your command."

"Answer me, O Lord, answer me, so these people will know that you, O Lord, are God, and that you are turning their hearts back again."

Then the fire of the Lord fell and burned up the sacrifice, the wood, the stones and the soil, and also licked up the water in the trench (1 Kings 18:36–38).

Elijah didn't have to put on a big show, because God was the star here. As Elijah stepped out of the way, God took center stage. Elijah's simple prayer accomplished more than all the gyrations of his enemy. Prayer is not about performance. It doesn't depend on the impressive words of the person praying. Prayer is all about the power of God moving from the heavenly realms and into the circumstances of earth.

Then Elijah turned to Ahab and said: "Go, eat and drink, for there is the sound of a heavy rain" (1 Kings 18:41). No one else could hear the sound of rain. Any one else listening in would likely say, "Pretty small chance!" Nothing in the environment had changed. It was dry as a bone and there were no clouds in the sky. Yet.

SMALL CLOUD, BIG RAINSTORM

Elijah knew not to be fooled by perceived size. He knew that nothing was small in God's hands. Elijah was praying at the top of Mt Carmel, powering the provision of God through the gap between heaven and earth. He prayed until he saw with his eyes what he had already seen with his heart.

Elijah was looking for a deluge so big that it might keep Ahab from being able to travel if he got caught in it. With his training in the power of small, when Elijah's eyes saw a cloud as small as a man's hand, his heart saw a drought-ending downpour.

DOWNPOUR

When God proclaimed the drought in Israel, its purpose was to bring His people back to Him. The drought was the first step on the way to the downpour.

Elijah was trained quietly, in hiding, in the ways of God and the power of small. He learned to see beyond what his eyes could perceive. He could see what no one else could because he was always alert to small indications that presaged God's downpour.

A CLOUD ON THE HORIZON

In 1921, a missionary couple named David and Svea Flood went with their two-year-old son from Sweden to the heart of Africa—to what was then called the Belgian Congo. They met up with another young Scandinavian couple, the Ericksons, and the four of them headed out to a remote area, leaving the relative safety of the main mission station.

Their experience was discouraging, with their only contact with villagers being a young boy who sold them chickens and eggs twice a week. Svea Flood decided that if this were her only contact, she would seek to lead him to Christ. In time, Svea gave birth to a daughter, and died in childbirth. Her husband, discouraged and bitter, left the newborn with the Ericksons and left the mission field, and turned his back on God altogether.

The Ericksons died shortly and the baby girl was handed over to some American missionaries who adjust her Swedish name to Aggie. They brought her to the United States and she grew up in South Dakota. She married Dewey Hurst, they had two children, and her husband became the president of a college in the Seattle area, where Aggie was exposed to local Scandinavian heritage. An article in a Swedish religious magazine led her to the discovery of her birth heritage.

The little boy her mother had led to the Lord had built a school in the village and led his students to Christ, who led their families to Christ. Eventually the village chief came to Christ.

A few years later, the Hursts were attending an evangelism conference in London, England, when a report was given from the nation of Zaire (the former Belgian Congo). The superintendent of the national church, representing some 110,000 baptized believers, spoke eloquently of the gospel's spread in his nation. Aggie could not help going to ask him afterward if he had ever heard of David and Svea Flood. "Yes, madam," the man replied in French, his words then being translated into English. "It was Svea Flood who led me to Jesus Christ. I was the boy who brought food to your parents before you were born. In fact, to this day your mother's grave and her memory are honored by all of us." (One Witness) http://jmm.aaa.net.au/articles/14168.htm

SMALL CHANGE

Be on the lookout for small encouragement. View it as your cloud as small as a man's hand. When you come across small inspiration, pray: "I see Your downpour."

DAY **24**

*"'Don't be afraid,' the prophet answered.
'Those who are with us are more than
those who are with them'"
(2 Kings 6:16).*

The prophet Elisha was a thorn in the side of the enemy king. Elisha received revelation from God about the King of Aram's plans, then disclosed those plans to the king of Israel. When the enemy forces realized how Israel was getting its intelligence, he made a plan to capture Elisha. To capture this one lone man and his one servant, "he sent horses and chariots and a strong force there. They went by night and surrounded the city" (2 Kings 6:14).

Horses, chariots, and a strong force on one side; Elijah and his servant on the other. Does that sound like a fair fight? It does if you know about the power of small.

> When the servant of the man of God got up and went out early the next morning, an army with horses and chariots had surrounded the city. "Oh, my lord, what shall we do?" the servant asked.
>
> "Don't be afraid," the prophet answered. "Those who are with us are more than those who are with them."
>
> And Elisha prayed, "O Lord, open his eyes so he may see." Then the Lord opened the servant's eyes, and he looked and saw the hills full of horses and chariots of fire all around Elisha (2 Kings 6:15–17).

Elisha could already see what his servant could not. Elisha's eyes were acclimated to the spiritual realm. He understood the power of small—what looks small to the physical senses has the big power and provision of God standing behind it. I think of it like the tip of an iceberg. All the power is right there, under the water. When you see the tip it alerts you to the presence of the iceberg. You know the tip isn't the whole picture.

Elisha looks around, sees himself and his servant, and realizes that they are just the tip of the iceberg.

WHAT YOU CAN'T SEE

> Therefore we do not lose heart. Though outwardly we are wasting away, yet inwardly we are being renewed day by day.

> For our light and momentary troubles are achieving for us
> an eternal glory that far outweighs them all.
>
> So we fix our eyes not on what is seen, but on what is
> unseen. For what is seen is temporary, but what is unseen
> is eternal (2 Corinthians 4:16–18).

Everything that you see in the physical realm is the tip of an iceberg. To the trained eye, it is immediately apparent that a whole realm of power and provision fill out the picture, if only we could see what God sees.

In the physical realm, your eyes have to adjust to changes in light. It takes a few minutes for your eyes to make the adjustment. Your pupils have to either expand or contract so that they are taking in the right amount of light. If you are thrust from darkness into light, there will be an adjustment period. When you suddenly find yourself blinded by the light, just stand still. Let the process of acclimating happen naturally. Suddenly you discover that there are all kinds of new things to see.

When you follow Paul's suggestion and fix your eyes on what is not seen, whatever you fix your eyes on soon becomes the point of emphasis against which everything else recedes.

I have a scratch on a piece of furniture in my living room. It's not a very big scratch and had possibly been there for years before I noticed it. Something brought it to my attention and now I can't help seeing it. Now it is the first thing I see when I look at that table. I imagine that everyone who might say, "What a lovely table," is really thinking, "Did you see that scratch?" My eyes are trained to see the scratch and it has grown huge in my sight.

Do your problems seem large and you small in comparison? Look around until you see the tip of the iceberg. Fix your eyes on it until it fills your sight. The power of small is never more in evidence than when your spiritual enemy looks big and imposing and overwhelming. Faith the size of a mustard seed has the power to move a mountain.

Elisha's eyes were trained. He knew just where to look. He was seeing what God was seeing. If we could see things the way God sees them—end from the beginning; all the parts in motion toward a goal— we would make the same decisions God makes. Any time it looks like God might be getting it wrong, stop and let your eyes adjust.

LEARNING TO SEE THE ANSWERS TO YOUR PRAYERS: ALIGNING YOURSELF WITH TRUTH

Several years ago, a woman came to me for prayer. She was desperate and afraid. Her son had been arrested for selling drugs. She told me the story of his years of drug abuse—the anguished attempts to overcome his addiction; the glimpses of hope that turned out to be false hope. Through his story she weaved her own: she had prayed every way she knew how and God had never answered. I sensed that she had come to me because she was looking for someone who knew how to pray with such skill that she could get God to behave as the woman thought He should. She had a long list of instructions for what I was to pray.

I began by asking her, "What is it that you really desire for your son?" As she went back to her list and began to read off her instructions for God, I interrupted her. "No. Those are the things that you have determined will accomplish what you really want for your son." Years ago, God taught me that I can't know the desire of my heart unless I know the heart of my desire. I helped her peel back the layers until she discovered the center of her desire: that her son would know Jesus Christ and find peace in his life. "That's what we'll ask for," I told her.

Things didn't go well, if you define reality by the circumstances. The evidence was overwhelming. Her son was bitter and suffering excruciating withdrawal. In her panic, she would say, "God isn't answering. Why isn't God doing anything?" I reminded her what we were praying for. "Change your perspective," I told her. "Don't say, 'God isn't answering'; instead, say, 'This is how God is answering. This is the path His yes is taking.'"

Fast-forward. He was given a prison sentence. I wish that I could tell you the details that had to fall into place for God's plan to emerge, but I will condense the story. He was led to Christ by a fellow inmate, who got him involved in a prison Bible study. Gradually, he became a different man. When he was paroled, he had to continue in a daily drug rehabilitation program. He finished the program, continued in his Christian walk, and has been sober and working for just over two years.

What appeared to be backward was really forward. What appeared to be down was really up. What appeared to be dark was really light.

THOSE WHO ARE WITH YOU

You don't have to wonder what the truth of a situation is. You can know. It is always so: Those who are with you are greater than those who are against you. Let that reality be as sure and certain for you as if your eyes could see them.

SMALL CHANGE

Reenvision every circumstance and problem as God sees them. When you become worried or anxious, pray: "He who is with me is greater than he who is with them." Let the eyes of your heart see clearly the power and provision of God that is the iceberg underneath the tip.

DAY **25**

"Are not two sparrows sold for a penny?
Yet not one of them will fall to the ground apart
from the will of your Father.
And even the very hairs of your head
are all numbered.
So don't be afraid; you are worth more
than many sparrows"
(Matthew 10:29–31).

The littlest, cheapest bird—a sparrow. That's what Jesus used to illustrate God's attention to the small. Even a worthless sparrow is an object of God's control. The hairs on your head! Do you know how complicated it could be to keep track of the hairs on your head? All those hairs have growth cycles. One hair is here today and gone tomorrow and back in a few months. It's not just numbering them once. It would require constant vigilance.

Jesus is being witty. He is finding the most outrageous way of illustrating your heavenly Father's constant attention to the details of your life. He is so careful over the smallest, most insignificant details of your life that His attention never wanders from you, day or night. Small details do not escape His provision.

The smallest details of your life are in His hands. I could tell you many stories about God's provision, but my favorite has to do with His kind supply of hairspray.

The Lord had called me to learn at deepest levels what He means in Matthew 6:33: "But seek first his kingdom and his righteousness, and all these things will be given to you as well." I was challenged to leave every single need is His hands and see what happened. One morning, I ran out of hairspray. I assure you that hairspray is a need in my life. I need the kind of hairspray that will form a shield against flying objects. Really need it.

That seems a simple thing, but the Lord seemed to say to me, "What about our experiment? What would happen if you let Me fulfill your need while you seek Me?" So, I determined that God wanted to supply hairspray if He agreed with my assessment about how much I needed it. My motto for that year was "If God doesn't supply it, then I don't need it."

That day a friend of mine, the late Jeannie Parrott, picked me up. She was in the middle of a move. "The company I work for makes hairspray," she said. "I buy it by the case. I don't want to move this case of hairspray so I brought it to you."

I laugh still when I tell the story. If God is going to supply me with hairspray, then surely He will supply me with everything I need. Could I have done ministry without hairspray? But, God delights in meeting the small needs to help us realize how attentive He is to our every cry. He dotes on us and keeps us as the apple of His eye.

TOUGH TIMES CALL FOR TOUGH FAITH

We are living in times that will certainly put this to the test. Traumatic prolonged unemployment; daily uncertainty; foreclosures; business closings. Tough times.

No one can promise you that you won't be hit by these kinds of disasters. In this world, you are guaranteed to have trouble. You may have a time of being stripped of both pride and possessions. But the promise of God is sure. He is right there and has been since before you knew disaster would hit. This has not happened in your life outside His loving and redemptive plan.

Sometimes people get angry with me when I say that. "How could you think that God had anything to do with this?" they might demand. My answer: Either God is in control, or we are on our own. Either God's Word is true and He is in control of our lives, or we're in relationship with a God who says, "Good luck with that." I believe with all my heart that God is a provider and that He provides in ways that lift us up, not tear us down.

I have lived in God's provision for many years and have, like Paul, learned to be content with plenty, and with little. I have seen God make specific provision just in time. I have also seen Him withhold the provision I thought I needed, but walk me step by step through the crisis. I've seen enough to know that whatever situation I find myself in, God is right there. He has gone ahead of me and He is bringing up the rear and He is present in me, working for me. Just take it as it comes.

I know that whatever He calls you to, He will provide for. He will do it sometimes in ways that will serve as markers for you. "If He will do this, then I know I can count on everything else I need." In *Forgotten God*, Francis Chan tells the following story.

> Years ago, Dave Phillips and his wife, Lynn, had a talk about the callings they felt God was stirring in them. As they discussed what they were most passionate about, they agreed

that bringing relief to suffering children and reaching the next generation with the gospel were at the top of the list. The thought of starting a relief agency was considered, but Dave's response was, "But that would mean I have to talk in front of people." By nature, Dave is a very quiet, behind-the-scenes man.

But after much prayer, Dave set aside his fears, and he and Lynn started Children's Hunger Fund out of their garage. Six weeks after CHF was launched, in January of 1992, he received a phone call from the director of a cancer treatment center in Honduras asking if there was any way he could obtain a certain drug for seven children who would die without it. Dave wrote down the name of the drug and told the director that he had no idea how to get this type of drug. They then prayed over the phone and asked God to provide.

As Dave hung up the phone, before he even let go of the receiver, the phone rang again. It was a pharmaceutical company in New Jersey asking Dave if he would have any use for 48,000 vials of that exact drug! Not only did they offer him eight million dollars' worth of this drug, but they told him they would airlift it anyplace in the world! Dave would later learn that the company was one of only two that manufactured this particular drug in the United States.

Within forty-eight hours, Dave had the drug sent to the treatment center in Honduras and to twenty other locations as well. It was then he believed that God was at work, validating his calling to this ministry.

Year after year, God continues to provide supernaturally. Today they have distributed more than $950 million in food and other relief to more than ten million kids in seventy countries and thirty-two states. Children's Hunger Fund has distributed more than 150 million pounds of food and 110 million toys.

Francis Chan, *Forgotten God* (David C. Cook, 2009), pp. 135–136

Do you see how God is working on your behalf in places where you don't see it or know it? But, at the ripe moment, it shows up. It has been in process all along, but it enters your experience as if it were sudden. Out of nowhere.

SMALL IS THE NEW BIG

We are reminded again of the power of small. God uses those small moments of intimacy and obedience to train us and get us ready for what comes next. Be faithful in the small so you can be given responsibility over much.

SMALL CHANGES

Let your anxiety turn you to faith. What small provision has He made for you today? Honor it. Let it grow big in your assessment. Think of the small provision and pray: "You are a big God."

DAY **26**

*"If you obey my commands, you will remain
in my love, just as I have obeyed my Father's
commands and remain in his love"
(John 15:10).*

I have mined these words for many years. This call fascinates me and woos me. Jesus offers the possibility and then makes it possible for me to obey Him the way He obeyed the Father, and so walk daily in the experience of His outrageous love for me, the same way He lived in an awareness and reality of the Father's love. I want it.

How did Jesus obey the Father? What was the power that empowered Jesus? The eternal Holy Spirit filled Him and led Him.

> Jesus, full of the Holy Spirit, returned from the Jordan and was led by the Spirit in the desert (Luke 4:1).

> Jesus returned to Galilee in the power of the Spirit, and news about him spread through the whole countryside (Luke 4:14).

> The scroll of the prophet Isaiah was handed to him. Unrolling it, he found the place where it is written: "The Spirit of the Lord is on me, because he has anointed me to preach good news to the poor. He has sent me to proclaim freedom for the prisoners and recovery of sight for the blind, to release the oppressed" (Luke 4:17–18).

> At that time Jesus, full of joy through the Holy Spirit, said, "I praise you, Father, Lord of heaven and earth, because you have hidden these things from the wise and learned, and revealed them to little children. Yes, Father, for this was your good pleasure" (Luke 10:21).

> You know what has happened throughout Judea, beginning in Galilee after the baptism that John preached—how God anointed Jesus of Nazareth with the Holy Spirit and power, and how he went around doing good and healing all who were under the power of the devil, because God was with him (Acts 10:37–38).

Are you getting the picture? Jesus acted in the power of the Spirit. That's how He heard from the Father and that's how He obeyed the Father and that's how the Father's love was communicated to His heart and mind. The same Spirit who empowered Jesus to obey the Father has been transfused into us by the same Jesus who did the obeying.

OBEDIENCE BY OBEDIENCE

So, again, how did Jesus obey the Father? Did He have a checklist of behaviors? The answer has to be that He obeyed the Father step by step, minute by minute, thought by thought, action by action.

Life is a whole lot of small. Have you noticed? Mostly minutia and details and ordinariness, punctuated by some drama here and there. If most of life is made up of small moments, then most of obedience must be made up of small obedience.

The same would have been true of Jesus' obedience. Because of His obedience in the moments of life that were unnoticed by others—His obedience behind the scenes in the private arena—when He encountered an incident that called for big obedience He was already in that flow. Big obedience was nothing more than a continuation of His life's trajectory.

"And being found in appearance as a man, he humbled himself and became obedient to death—even death on a cross!" (Philippians 2:8). The Cross was the pinnacle of His obedience. It was the completion of His hand-to-hand combat against sin.

> "Consider him who endured such opposition from sinful men, so that you will not grow weary and lose heart. In your struggle against sin, you have not yet resisted to the point of shedding your blood" (Hebrews 12:3–4).

He resisted sin—fought it fiercely—to the point of shedding blood.

The Crucifixion was the event that changed everything for everybody forever. I don't think I can overstate the case. I think I can use all the all-inclusive words and still not quite hit the mark. It was huge. But it was the culmination of a whole lot of small.

What empowered the final great obedience? "How much more, then, will the blood of Christ, who *through the eternal Spirit* offered himself unblemished to God, cleanse our consciences from acts that lead to death, so that we may serve the living God!" (Hebrews 9:14, emphasis added).

The Holy Spirit enabled Jesus' obedience from beginning to end. Little things, big things, bigger things, and the biggest thing—all Spirit-powered.

THE SPIRIT'S LASER BEAM

As Jesus walked out His days in obedience to the Father, led and filled by the Spirit, He happened upon people who might easily have been lost in the crowd except that the Spirit pointed them out. It amazes me to think about the many times when Jesus noticed the unnoticed and zeroed in on the least likely. Was He just quirky like that? Or is that how it often looks to obey Jesus like Jesus obeyed the Father? Do those who are small in society's estimation loom large in the Father's eyes?

Consider the lame man whom Jesus healed in John 5:1–8. Jesus was in Jerusalem for a feast—probably the Feast of Tabernacles. This was a pilgrim feast—all Jews who could do so were to be present in Jerusalem. So, it was a rowdy, loud, crowded time in Jerusalem. We find Jesus in a location called the pool of Bethesda, where legend and superstition held that the angels would trouble the water and the first to enter it would be healed.

This location was likely not Jesus' destination. He is most likely to have cut through it on His way elsewhere. It was a location jam-packed with people in need, none of them seeking out Jesus. But Jesus showed up anyway.

I think Jesus never considered His path to be just a shortcut or a convenience. I think He was always alert for the Spirit's spotlight to fall on someone that just happened to be on His way.

A woman at a well in Samaria. A widowed mother on her way to bury her only son. A man with a palsied hand. A beggar who had been blind from birth. And, the lame man at the Pool of Bethesda.

They didn't call out to Jesus, but Jesus called out to them. Why? What called Jesus' attention to these invisible lost causes?

Jesus answered that question for us. Jesus gave them this answer:

> "I tell you the truth, the Son can do nothing by himself; he can do only what he sees his Father doing, because whatever the Father does the Son also does. For the Father loves the Son and shows him all he does" (John 5:19–20).

He was obeying the Father.

Notice this description of the situation: "Here *a great number of disabled people* used to lie—the blind, the lame, the paralyzed. *One who was there* had been an invalid for thirty-eight years" (John 5:3–5, emphasis added). Do you see it? Out of the great number, the Spirit focused Jesus on one man. One pitiful, useless man. Abandoned by everyone, all alone. Jesus saw the man who was just part of the everyday scenery to others, and took the man's brokenness and misery away in the span of a few minutes.

A WHOLE LOT OF SMALL

D o you see how Jesus obeyed the Father? In the moment. He lived on the alert to the Spirit's leading. He kept His eyes peeled for what the Father was doing. And, He invites us to obey Him the same way.

SMALL CHANGE

S urrender to the Spirit's leading moment by moment. Ask the Father to talk really loud if you are spiritually hard of hearing. Be aware of kindnesses you can gift to those around you as you go.

DAY **27**

"Night and day, whether he sleeps or gets up,
the seed sprouts and grows,
though he does not know how"
(Mark 4:27).

Let's return to the seed metaphor because it is one that the Scripture uses over and over. God's kingdom works on a principle that I call "the principle of progressive revelation." If you look closely at God's work from Genesis through Revelation, His work in your life, His work in the lives of others, you will see that nothing springs forth full-grown. Everything in the material creation and everything in the spiritual realm is progressively revealed. For this reason, it requires both faith and patience to receive your inheritance—the promises.

> "We do not want you to become lazy, but to imitate those who
> through faith and patience inherit what has been promised.
> . . . And so after waiting patiently, Abraham received what
> was promised" (Hebrews 6:12, 15).

Faith is the ability to know for certain what you cannot observe with your physical senses. (See Hebrews 11:1.) The word translated "patience" is more accurately translated "longsuffering." It suggests a tranquil soul, a sedate mind, an unruffled attitude toward difficulty, a steadiness of purpose.

The promises that are your inheritance—your certain possession— will not come into your life full-grown. The promises to which the writer of Hebrews is referring are not generic promises, but specific promises to individuals. God promised Abraham specifically: "'I will surely bless you and give you many descendants'" (Hebrews 6:14). Yet this promise was progressively unfolded. God did not make the promise and fulfill the promise on the same day. A long period of time elapsed between the promise and its fulfillment. Abraham had to exercise faith and patience before the fulfillment of the promise entered his experience.

Abraham's faith journey was much like the farmer's experience in Jesus' parable. When the seed was planted—when Abram entered into covenant with God and combined his faith with God's promise—a long period ensued that appeared from the earth perspective to be desultory. Weeks, months, years, decades passed with no sign of the promised heir. God was working. We see it clearly in retrospect. But His work was underground; His work was invisible to the physical eye. Yet that period of invisible activity was bringing about exactly the right setting, exactly the right time, and exactly the right heart to put the Promise on the earth at the opportune moment. When that moment arrived, that exactly right predetermined moment, the stalk appeared—Isaac was born. Then the head appeared—the nation of Israel grew more numerous than the sands on the seashore or the stars in the sky. Then the full kernel in the head—the Messiah was born and brought salvation and redemption.

Abraham was "still living by faith when [he] died. [He] did not receive the things promised; [he] only saw them and welcomed them from a distance" (Hebrews 11:13). Abraham received what was promised directly to him—an heir and a land—but he did not receive the full kernel in the head, the fully developed promise.

For you and me it is different. The whole harvest is ripe. We only have to put the sickle to it. We only have to harvest the ripe promises, all of which have found their yes in Christ. However, those promises will still enter our lives in the same way that God's promise to Abraham entered his life. First the seed, then the waiting and training period during which we exercise faith and patience, then the stalk, the head, and finally, the full kernel in the head. This is God's pattern and He never deviates from it. He never acts like a vending machine or an instant "scratch-and-win" game. His purpose is too far-reaching, His plans are too long-term, His riches are too precious for Him to throw them at us like confetti. He must prepare the ground in which the promise will grow. As the fulfilled promises appear in our experience, they are well-rooted and fully nourished because of the faith and patience that has fertilized them.

When the farmer plants the seed, the harvest is a foregone conclusion. When God's specific promises come into your life the fulfillment is a foregone conclusion. He performs with His hand what He promises with His mouth. He keeps covenant. It is impossible for Him to lie. The farmer could miss the harvest only one way: by leaving his field behind. He might grow impatient with the process and decide that the seed would not really produce the plant. He might imagine that he could get a quicker harvest somewhere else. He might decide that it's easier to buy someone else's harvest instead of waiting on his own.

The harvest would still come, but he would not be there to put the sickle to it.

GOD'S INVISIBLE WORK

It's easy for us to misunderstand the interaction between the spiritual realm—the invisible aspects of reality—and the material and physical realm—the tangible aspects of reality. Our impression might be that God's work in the material realm, His work in getting the promise into our earthly experience, is the primary work. This thinking is exactly the reverse of the truth. The earth belongs to God. He created it and He sustains it. He is sovereign over all the earth. The warfare and the work does not occur in the material realm. Putting His resources into our lives at precisely the right time and in precisely the right way presents no difficulty for Him. He does not need our help. The warfare and the work occur in the spiritual realm. He has ordained prayer as the way we will cooperate with Him as He does His spiritual, inside, underground work. As soon as the spiritual work is done, the material manifestation of the promise appears on earth.

This time of unobservable work, this time during which the seed is germinating, is a time of activity and a time in which God's power is operating mightily. We will only know this work by faith because faith is what connects our earthly minds to spiritual reality. Don't mistake the appearance of inactivity for God's delay. He is not delaying; He is working in the invisible realm.

BLIND SIGHT

James Pence wrote a novel titled *Blind Sight*. The main character was a man whose family had been killed, and who was angry with God. James was disappointed in the sales and discouraged. However, through circumstances unknown to James, his novel was about to change a life.

At 3:00 A.M. on March 1, 2008, Terry Caffey's life changed forever. Two young men—one of them his daughter Erin's ex-boyfriend— entered the Caffey house and shot Terry, his wife, Penny, and their two sons, Matthew and Tyler, then set fire to the house. Terry regained consciousness and escaped his burning house. He crawled nearly 400 yards to a neighbor's home, even though he had been shot at least five times at close range. In the hospital later, he learned that his daughter had been implicated in the murders. Terry became suicidal, feeling as if he'd lost all reason to live. He gave up on life.

Upon visiting his burned-out property, Terry noticed a scorched scrap of paper from one of his wife's books leaning against a tree trunk. The page read:

> "[God,] I couldn't understand why You would take my family and leave me behind to struggle along without them. And I guess I still don't totally understand that part of it. But I do believe that You're sovereign; You're in control."

That page was like a direct message from God, and it turned Terry's life around. It was a scrap of a page from James Pence's novel, *Blind Sight.*

A seed that fell into the ground to die, but produced a great harvest. Now, Terry has remarried, is the adoptive father of two young sons, and is rebuilding his relationship with his 17-year-old daughter Erin, who is currently serving two life sentences in a Texas state penitentiary for her involvement in the crimes. http://terrycaffey.com/?page_id=113 http://jamespence.com/?page_id=83

GET SMALL

John the Baptist, with Jesus in view, remarked, "He must become greater; I must become less" (John 3:30) Do you see how small needs to be our goal?

> If You chose the lowliest of men to hear the announcement of heaven's proudest moment, then make me lowly. I choose not to seek the praise of people, but rather to crave the lowliest place, from which I can hear You clearly. To bow at Your feet is my highest aspiration. Here is where I can hear the song of the ages: glory to God and peace to people on earth. (*Pursuing the Christ*)

SMALL CHANGE

Instead of trying to promote yourself, deliberately promote others. The Lord will bring you up to the head of the table when He decides to do so. Notice how your flesh responds to promoting others. As you do, pray: "You, Lord, become greater while I become less."

DAY **28**

We have reached the end of our 28-day journey. How have you changed? What is the most significant small change you have made?

How have you become aware of as a cloud as small as a man's hand? The hint of what is to come?

How have you redefined some of your circumstances by remembering that you only see the tip of the iceberg?

How will you deliberately become less while He becomes greater?

How has your perspective changed through your 28-day journey focusing on the power of small?

THINK SMALL
LIVE LARGE

THINK SMALL, LIVE LARGE

Books by
Jennifer Kennedy Dean

**The Life-Changing
Power in the
Name of Jesus**
978-1-56309-841-3

Secrets Jesus Shared
*Kingdom Insights Revealed
Through the Parables*
978-1-59669-108-7

Set Apart
*A 6-Week Study
of the Beatitudes*
978-1-59669-263-3

Heart's Cry
Principles of Prayer
978-1-59669-095-0

Life Unhindered!
Five Keys to Walking in Freedom
978-1-59669-286-2

Live a Praying Life!
*Open Your Life to God's
Plan and Provision*
978-1-59669-299-2